New Library of Pastoral Care

Swift to Hear

hael Jacobs is Director of the Counselling and
chotherapy programme and senior lecturer at the
iversity of Leicester. He is a Fellow of the British
ciation of Counselling and a UKCP registered psy-
otherapist. His other books in this series include a
cond edition of *Still Small Voice*, and *Holding in Trust*;
ther major texts which he has published include *The
resenting Past* (Open University Press) and
sychodynamic Counselling in Action* (Sage), both in
second editions.

New Library of Pastoral Care

STILL SMALL VOICE
An Introduction to Pastoral
Counselling
Michael Jacobs

MAKE OR BREAK
An Introduction to Marriage
Counselling
Jack Dominian

BRIEF ENCOUNTERS
Pastoral Ministry through Baptisms,
Weddings and Funerals
Wesley Carr

LOVE THE STRANGER
Ministry in Multi-Faith Areas
Roger Hooker and Christopher Lamb

BEING THERE
Care in Time of Illness
Peter Speck

CRISIS COUNSELLING
Caring for People in Emotional
Shock
Howard Stone

LIFE CYCLES
Women and Pastoral Care
*Elaine Graham and
Margaret Halsey (eds)*

LETTING GO
Caring for the Dying
and the Bereaved
*Ian Ainsworth-Smith and
Peter Speck*

GOING SOMEWHERE
People with Mental Handicaps and
their Pastoral Care
Sheila Hollins and Margaret Grimer

MADE IN HEAVEN?
Ministry with Those Intending
Marriage
Peter Chambers

HELPING THE HELPERS
Supervision and Pastoral Care
John Foskett and David Lyall

CLERGY STRESS
The Hidden Conflicts in Ministry
Mary Anne Coate

HOLDING IN TRUST
The Appraisal of Ministry
Michael Jacobs

BEING YOUR AGE
Pastoral Care for Older People
Michael Butler and Ann Orbach

SIN, GUILT AND FORGIVENESS
The Hidden Dimensions of a Pastoral
Process
Mary Anne Coate

SOCIOLOGY FOR PASTORAL
CARE
George Furniss

A DICTIONARY OF
PASTORAL CARE
edited by Alastair V. Campbell

NEW·LIBRARY·OF

PASTORAL·CARE

GENERAL EDITOR: WESLEY CARR

SWIFT TO HEAR

*Facilitating Skills in Listening
and Responding*

Michael Jacobs

First edition published in Great Britain 1985 (nine impressions)
Second edition published 2000
SPCK
Holy Trinity Church
Marylebone Road
London NW1 4DU

British Library Cataloguing-in-Publication Data

A catalogue record for this book is available
from the British Library

ISBN 0–281–05260–3

Typeset by Pioneer Associates, Perthshire
Printed in Great Britain by
The Cromwell Press, Trowbridge, Wiltshire

'Be swift to hear, slow to speak'
(James 1.19)

Contents

Contents

Contents

Foreword

The New Library of Pastoral Care is designed for those who are interested in pastoral care and who wish to improve their knowledge and skills. As general editor of the series I hope that it will prove useful both to clergy and laity, as well as to those outside the churches who wish to learn something of the role of the pastor.

Learning for pastoral care has always drawn from contemporary secular knowledge. Today aspects of social work, counselling, psychotherapy and community development inform its understanding of men and women. Particular value, for instance, might derive from a grasp of the social context of the pastoral task, the dynamics of the helping relationship and the attitudes and skills which make for effective pastoral interventions. Learning through practice is becoming increasingly important. Knowledge does not stand still. Those interested in the field, therefore, may struggle to keep up with new developments and to sort out which ideas and practices are relevant to their pastoral activity. Volumes in the series always introduce theory in the context of practice. Occasional volumes of Study Resources cover a specific field in more depth.

There is still some anxiety that by acquiring wider learning pastors may lose their grasp of their pastoral identity and abandon their distinctive theological discipline. They may then become 'just another' social worker or counsellor. It does not detract from the value of these professions to assert that the role of the pastor is unique and deserves to be clarified and strengthened. The two recurrent themes in this series are the pastor's theological commitment and his or her specific role. Yet pastors do not work in a vacuum. They need to be able to co-operate with those in other disciplines whose work may overlap with their own. Those among whom they minister have been brought up in a society in which behavioural assumptions are prominent. Such ministry requires awareness of a range of shared concepts and language.

Within the various church traditions there is a rich variety of styles of and approaches to pastoral work. No attempt is made in this series to reduce these to uniformity. Some volumes will be more specifically theological and others more concerned with practice. All, however, attempt to hold these two referents in mind. I hope that the series will prove informative and stimulating across all boundaries, whether of denomination or of psychological and sociological theory.

Wesley Carr

Preface to the
Second Edition

Since the first edition of *Swift to Hear* there have been significant changes in the way we understand the plural society in which we live – changes which necessitate extending the examples in this book to include a more comprehensive cross-section of the population. Following its publication I have written a number of other books, as well as revised *Still Small Voice* which is now in a second edition. I have produced further exercises in listening and responding, and other exercises to develop the basic skills and broaden the ways in which counsellors, and those who use counselling skills, can work with people. When my book *Insight and Experience* (1991, Open University Press) went out of print, this revision of *Swift to Hear* provided the opportunity to include the most relevant of its exercises in this edition.

Expanding the book in this way made it seem a natural move to cut out the former chapters on small groups and on large groups. I hope to write another book in this series on group work, in which I can expand the original chapters, with other material on groups from *Insight and Experience*.

However much my ideas and practice of counselling and therapy have developed since the first edition of *Swift to Hear*, I return time and again to the basic skills, for which there really is no substitute. There is clearly much need for more knowledge and practice of these skills, without always having to go into the more complex situations of pastoral counselling. We have learned how to identify basic skills more clearly, and produced different ways of teaching and practising them. But good listening, and accurate, empathic, and insightful responding remain as central as ever they were. I trust that this edition builds upon all that was true in the first, corrects some of the imbalance there may have been there, but above all promotes better relating between individuals. It is a truism, but none the less important for that, that we would all do well to listen more. It is the type of listening that matters. And although it may equally be true that we should learn to say less, we also need to learn how to respond, because a good response shows not just how well we have listened, but that we have something valuable to give in return.

This book stands in its own right, but it is also a primer for *Still Small Voice*. In no way would I wish to give the impression, as far as counselling goes (including pastoral counselling), that the practitioner stops here. Many of the deeper, and more important issues are dealt with in *Still Small Voice*, including further dimensions of helping which we need to know about, even if we do not see ourselves as formal counsellors and therapists.

I am grateful to a number of people for ideas which I have adapted in designing exercises. Peter Trower initially suggested that my teaching materials would make a book, and triggered off the writing of the first edition; his book, *Social Skills and Mental Health*, gave me some material for Exercise 6. Donald Anders-Richards, Gunna Dietrich, the late Alan Lilley, Sonia Ponter, and the late Maureen Wheeler suggested exercises which have appeared in both editions; and members of the Leicester Counselling Centre worked on the problem of how to practise the asking of questions. I am grateful to my wife Moira Walker for some of the role plays she has written, which highlight issues such as culture and disability, and which are included for the first time in this new edition.

Michael Jacobs
1999

ONE

Introducing the Basic Guidelines

———

Are we a caring society? The answer is complex. On the one hand, there are many people who engage in caring for others. Some are trained professionals in what used to be called vocational work. Some of these are paid well for their skills, while many others earn a living, but cannot be said to gain much financial reward for devoting their working lives to the welfare of patients, clients or users of their services. Many more carers are unpaid volunteers, although the term 'volunteer' is in some ways not right, because it fails to indicate the dedication as well as the professional attitude that is learned in training and is exercised in practice. This book is written for many of these carers, as well as for those who use counselling skills in their professional lives, to support their training in the use of listening and responding skills, as well as in the development of more advanced counselling skills.

On the other hand, if we look at those who are cared for by these people, and the organizations, institutions, charities and local groups for whom they work, we might be led to argue that we live in a very uncaring society, because many of those whom they help – patients, clients and users – have experienced at some point in their lives a profound lack of care. Those who offer care also need people to care for; and of these there are plenty, suffering in one way or another, temporarily or through a lifelong legacy, from relationships which have not provided the care we might have expected of families, of institutions, of commercial and business enterprises – and indeed the care we might have expected of society itself.

There is a further complexity to modern life. We have opportunities for the speediest of communications, we have political and religious leaders who can broadcast their ideas at the flick of a switch – and they, and we, have control of plenty of buttons which enable people to communicate across the world in fractions of a second. Yet for all the speed and craft of mass communication, or of personal communication through digital technology, as well as the public exposure to which people put themselves through the media, there are many other areas of life and many day-to-day situations in which it has become less easy for people to speak to each other.

My purpose in this book is to return to some basic rules of communication, so that those who offer care and counsel, and those who exercise leadership – in church or charity, in small groups or in larger organizations, in people's homes or in professional offices – can be encouraged to listen better, to respond more carefully, and to understand more clearly the experience, the thoughts and the feelings of others. Clergy and lay people, teachers and managers, doctors and nurses, youth leaders and social workers, spend much of their professional lives communicating with others – although too often it is what *they* need to communicate that appears to matter most. There is much to be learned from the training of those in the 'listening professions' (counsellors and therapists) which, apart from its importance to entering those professions, whether as salaried staff or unpaid volunteers, is also of value to those who work in related fields. A basic grounding for caring work involves learning about receiving communications as well as delivering them, and about listening and responding in such a way as obviates the necessity of having to take the lead and offer advice.

There are a number of relatively simple ground rules which people sometimes naturally use, without particular instruction – although seldom use enough unless it is pointed out how valuable they are. These I spell out in this book, although not in any simplistic way. Good communication may not in itself be enough, because people's situations are often far from simple, and they often need particular types of help and information. This book provides a basis for caring work; many people will need further specialist knowledge if they intend to use this basis to move into pastoral work, grief counselling, money advice, relationship conciliation and all the other areas of care which are so abundant in our society. Conversely, specialized knowledge is of little value unless the carer also listens to the one in need, and knows how to draw out the picture sufficiently in order to be able to offer their particular expertise. The simple rules set out in this chapter and developed through this book form a foundation for many kinds of helping interview, whether of a formal nature, or of that more informal type we tend to call a conversation. In some of the most straightforward requests for help, the skills of listening and responding often provide sufficient basis for people to express their feelings, to share their troubled thoughts, and then find their way through to their own resolution.

The guidelines I describe and illustrate through a series of exercises are perhaps rules for good communication, but they are not inviolable laws. In the early stages of practice particular ways of responding can appear artificial and contrived, although experience suggests that applying them in real situations yields results (in terms of openness of communication), which soon validates them. Taken one by one, as they are in this book, may make them appear too simple for words; but putting them into practice together in one interview (Chapter 4) is less easy. At first, both in practice ('role-play') situations and in real life, these guidelines assist the helper to monitor an interview or a conversation, partly at the time it takes place, but also when reflecting upon it afterwards. These guidelines can become second nature, although even the most experienced of helpers, if they become over-confident or too pressed by the demands of the work, can lose touch with the basic tools of good communication.

This book is set out as a text for training courses, for the benefit of those who conduct such training as well as those who learn from it. The exercises have proved useful in preparing people for pastoral visiting, in advice work, in training line managers, and even in teaching itself, for developing the interactive skills of schoolchildren and students. The nature of personal communication, which demands that there is one person who is in contact with at least one other, makes it impossible for this book to be read on its own, isolated from a training group, except as a way of preparing for, or reflecting upon, practical experience. Most people like to think they are better at listening and responding than in fact they are, and it is difficult to monitor oneself, unless a tape recorder is used (with the permission of the client) to play back an interview, or, as in a role play, another or others can observe it.

The guidelines are explained simply, and are in most instances illustrated with relatively straightforward exercises, which to be effective need be practised in the company of at least three or four other people. Since observers in such a small group will also know what to look for, they can provide invaluable comments upon each person's practice.

Exercise 1

Set out below are two pairs of interviews, or what might be described as conversations with a purpose. One pair is between a street warden from the local church and a new resident, and the other pair is between a line manager and an employee. They both illustrate the way in which effective listening and reflection can facilitate the making of a difficult decision, with the helper having to do little more than provide supportive or empathic comments, offering minimum support and advice. In each pair one script illustrates how badly an interview can go wrong if the responses are poor, if the helper is too active or judgemental, if there is inadequate reflection upon what has been said, and if there is misunderstanding or even a complete refusal to listen.

The scripts can be used to role-play the conversations out loud, since this reflects the tone of voice (something that the printed word cannot adequately convey). There are also recordings of these and other pairs of interviews available, which can be used instead of a live performance.[1] During and after each of the pairs of interviews, participants and observers should make notes about what they consider to be helpful and unhelpful responses. After discussion these observations can be compared with the suggestions that follow the scripts below.

Interview 1a

PAULA   Hello?
VISITOR   I'm the street warden from the church. I'm just calling because I noticed you recently moved into the road. I wanted to introduce myself to you and see if there's anything you need – you know, information about the area – that sort of thing.
PAULA   Thank you. I'm not sure there's anything . . . But come in a moment . . .
VISITOR   Are you sure? I needn't keep you long unless there's anything I can do to help.
PAULA   I'm not sure there is . . . Though I must say people aren't that friendly round here, not compared to where we came from.
VISITOR   I'm sorry to hear that. Have you moved far?

PAULA	Quite a way. My partner went for this new job and so I had to come . . .
VISITOR	That's hard . . . You didn't have much say in that?
PAULA	Well, you don't do you? It was a good opening for him, more money, but . . . [*Falls silent*]
VISITOR	But as far as you were concerned . . .?
PAULA	Yes – for me it wasn't so good. I had to leave my little job; it was in such a friendly firm.
VISITOR	And round here it doesn't feel friendly . . .
PAULA	No, it doesn't, you're right there.
VISITOR	I imagine it's difficult to feel very good about people when you're not sure you want to be here.
PAULA	I suppose that's it. It's not like me to feel down, but I have been feeling ever so low since we moved in.
VISITOR	It sounds as if you've had to leave behind friends, a nice job, your own life, for the sake of your partner . . .
PAULA	I don't blame him . . . I mean, it was a good move for him.
VISITOR	But for the moment I guess it doesn't feel such a good one for you.
PAULA	Well . . . [*Falls silent*]
VISITOR	Do you want to tell me a bit more about what you miss from your old home? I mean, I don't want to intrude, but . . .
PAULA	No, it would be nice to tell you a bit about it. I miss my friends I used to chat to . . . I think if I was more myself I might feel a bit more like getting to know people here. Do you know, one of the differences I've noticed about this area is that . . .

Interview 1b

PAULA	Hello?
VISITOR	I'm the street warden from the church. I'm just calling because I noticed you recently moved into the road. I wanted to introduce myself to you and

	see if there's anything we can do for you. There's lots of things going on at the local church . . .
PAULA	Thank you. I'm not sure there's anything. You see I'm not religious . . .
VISITOR	That doesn't matter. Can I come in? It won't take long. There's just a few things to tell you.
PAULA	I'm not sure . . . but if you want to.
VISITOR	Thank you. Oh, this is nice, isn't it? You *have* settled in well. It's pleasant round here, isn't it?
PAULA	I suppose so. Actually I didn't want to move here, but my partner went for this new job, so I had to.
VISITOR	You do have to go where your husband goes, don't you? One of the drawbacks of being a woman, isn't it, really?
PAULA	It was a good opening for him, more money, but . . . [*Falls silent*]
VISITOR	That'll be nice, won't it? Bit more to spend . . . Nice house too.
PAULA	I suppose so. I had to leave my little job; it was in such a friendly firm.
VISITOR	I expect you'll soon get another one. There are quite a lot of part-time openings round here, you know.
PAULA	Maybe . . . though I don't feel like applying for anything at present.
VISITOR	Oh, you will in time, when you're a bit more settled. It takes time, you know. I found that when I moved here. But I must say our little church is a very friendly place. You'd like it.
PAULA	[*switches off*] Mm . . .
VISITOR	There's a nice family service, just right for the children.
PAULA	We haven't got any children.
VISITOR	Oh, what a shame. It's so much easier settling in with children, isn't it? You know, you meet other mothers at the school, and . . .
PAULA	Well . . . [*Falls silent*]
VISITOR	Let me tell you a bit more about what we have at the church. You'll be able to meet people there very easily . . .

PAULA   Well, I don't want to be rude, but perhaps another time. I must get on. There's still lots of things to get straight. I'm sure you understand . . .

Interview 2a

MANAGER   Come in, Jones . . . Sit down over there . . . Now, what's all this about? I hear you've handed in your resignation . . . Seems rather a rash thing to do.

JACK   That's right, sir. Yes, I want to resign.

MANAGER   What on earth makes you want to do that? Are you not happy here? You've only got to tell me what's bugging you. Has someone been getting at you? That's the trouble with that new man who's joined your team, isn't it? He's a bit of a character, I could tell that when I interviewed him, but perhaps he gets up some people's noses. Look, you've been working long enough for us. I wouldn't have thought somebody like him would put you off.

JACK   It's not that . . .

MANAGER   Got another job? Better pay than here? We've had it tough recently I know, what with the recession, and foreign competition, and all that. They can't give you chaps as much as they'd like to . . . though things are looking up a bit now. Perhaps I could get you put up a grade. Would that help?

JACK   No, no, it's not that. I just want to resign. I don't really want to talk about it.

MANAGER   Now come on, Jack, you can tell me anything; we've known each other for some years, haven't we? We're mates. How long have you been with us? Let's see. [*Looks at papers*]
Eight years. That's not bad these days. You've got a good record. You're reliable – I don't remember you ever missing a day. You don't want to leave us, surely? I'll give you a good reference of course . . . but that's not what you want really, is it?

JACK   Yes . . . no . . . yes . . . I don't think you . . . look I'm sorry, but I've just got to. It's . . . er . . . well, it's . . . um . . . it's a family matter.

MANAGER	[*a bit taken aback. Short silence*] Well, in that case, you want to hang on to a job, you know. I mean . . . these days . . . I don't need to tell you about the employment situation – rather the unemployment situation . . . bit nearer the truth. [*Begins to recover confidence*] I remember when I first started here, well, you could almost choose any job you wanted. I mean, I get fed up with the job too sometimes, Jack. I know how it feels . . . I wouldn't give up a secure job if I were you.
JACK	Well, I don't think . . . I don't really want to. It's more . . . well, I've got to . . . it's the kids . . .
MANAGER	The kids? What have they got to do with it?
JACK	[*pauses, angry*] It's not something I really want to talk about.
MANAGER	[*impatient*] Well, you've told me that much, you might as well tell me the rest. Are they in trouble with the law? [*Looks at papers*] No, they can't be old enough yet.
JACK	[*equally impatient*] No, it's not that at all. [*Sighs*] Well . . . my partner's walked out. I'm left with the kids, and they need me. They need me at home. I've got to look after them, I've got to look after the place. And, well . . . it's just impossible after a long day's work, and overtime, and then you have to go back, and, well, honestly, it's just bedlam . . .
MANAGER	But look here, I mean, well, resigning's the last thing to do if you're concerned about your kids. You've got a steady job, you need it if you're going to provide for them. Can't you pay some woman to come in and look after them? Or what about social services? I'm sure they'll be able to help. Why don't you call in a social worker?
JACK	No. I'm not having anyone else look after them.
MANAGER	But can't you see? It's better to have a job. How are you going to manage on social security? I mean, we'll do what we can to help; perhaps I can get you a

special allowance or something. I can't promise anything, but, damn it all, it's a bit foolish to jack it all in.

JACK   Look here, I'm prepared to give up my job if it means I can look after the kids better. They don't have their mum there. It's the least I can do to make sure their dad's around when they need me.

MANAGER   Well, I understand the problem, of course. But I do think you're acting like a fool . . .

JACK   Look, that may be your opinion, but it's not mine. It's the only thing I can do. I'm going. Thank you for listening. I'm sorry to let you down like this . . . but there's no other way out.

MANAGER   Well, if you've made your mind up, I can see I'm not going to be able to change it. But I'm sorry to lose you, Jack. Best of luck to you. Thanks for coming in to see me. Close the door on the way out, will you?

Interview 2b

MANAGER   Come in Jack. Let's sit over there, shall we?
            [*Pause*]
            Now, I gather you want to resign your job.

JACK   Yes. That's right.

MANAGER   [*slight pause*] I'd be sorry to lose you. What's the reason?

JACK   Rather not say, Bill. I don't want to talk now . . .

MANAGER   It's sort of too personal, is it?

JACK   Yes, that's right.

MANAGER   Not the sort of thing it's easy to tell me.

JACK   Well . . . not really . . . I . . . well . . . no . . .

MANAGER   Go on, if you want to. Sometimes it's good to talk. I may be able to help.

JACK   Well, it's . . .
            [*Sighs*]
            It's home.

MANAGER   [*short silence*] Home?

JACK   Yes . . . yes . . . My partner's walked out . . . Left me with the kids.

MANAGER	That must have been a real shock.
JACK	Well, I half expected it, really. Sorry to let you down, Bill.
MANAGER	It sounds like you're the one who's been let down, Jack.
JACK	[*bitter*] Not half.
	[*Short silence*]
MANAGER	So your partner's walked out, left you with the kids, and you want to resign.
JACK	[*sighs*] I wish I could see a way out, but . . . you know what it's like.
MANAGER	They're youngsters, aren't they?
JACK	Yes, poor things. Well, I mean, who's going to get them off to school, who's going to meet them? I'm knackered after a day at work and overtime. I can't cope with my job and look after them. I don't want to let *them* down. And I might lose them if I wasn't looking after them properly. Someone's got to keep the house, play with them, feed them . . . I've just got to be there.
MANAGER	[*pause*] So it's difficult to have to come into work?
JACK	No, not really. Well, I mean, it's good to see my mates, and at the moment it would be something to take my mind off it. It's awful being on your own all day when the kids are at school . . . But honestly, I can't see how I can cope with both.
MANAGER	So the stress has been getting you down?
JACK	Yes . . .
MANAGER	[*pause*] Mm . . .
	[*Jack hesitates and then sighs*]
MANAGER	I get the feeling you're having to give up the job, but you're not really sure you want to. You can't see a way of doing a good day's work here, and being a good dad to your kids.
JACK	That's just it. I don't know what to do.
MANAGER	So you'd like to keep your job, but there's no way you can do that and be at home when the kids need you.
JACK	I wish there was some way . . .
MANAGER	Could there be?
JACK	Well, I did wonder whether I could work a shorter

	day. But then if my mates found out what had happened, well, they might blame me in some way. They know I work hard, and I know I'm not the life and soul of the party, so they might think that's why my partner's walked out on me. Anyway, I'd earn less, and probably get more on benefit.
MANAGER	So there's another problem: what your mates would say . . . Then there's the money.
JACK	Well, the money's not the end of the world. I'd like to work, I always have worked. But my mates . . .
MANAGER	So you're worried that they'll see you just as a hard worker and won't understand what went wrong. Perhaps your partner didn't understand . . .?
JACK	[*angry*] At least my mates know me better than her.
MANAGER	Look, Jack, I can see it's not easy. But sometimes people act a bit, well, on impulse, especially when they've had a shock to the system. Now if I could arrange a shorter day for you on the same money – just for a while – that might help you see how things go at home and here with your mates. If it doesn't work, we can think again, and if you still feel you have to, well you could resign then instead of making a hasty decision now. What do you feel about that?
JACK	I don't know really . . . It's . . . possible . . .
MANAGER	Well, take a bit of time to think about it. If you want to you can knock off early today . . . I'll fix that. Come back in a couple of days. We can talk some more. You can tell me about things at home if you want to.
JACK	That sounds reasonable. Okay, Bill . . . Look, I'm sorry to be so much trouble.
MANAGER	It sounds like you're the one who's got a fair share of troubles at the moment . . .

Opinions inevitably differ about what makes for good or bad interviewing, and if the scenes are being played out in the group, each person's tone of voice will also have some bearing on whether or not a particular response sounds helpful. Below are various points that have been raised in discussion groups which have played out one or both of these pairs of interviews, or have listened to the taped version. These points can be compared with the lists generated in your own discussions. While it is fairly straightforward to spot poor interviewing techniques, there are many ways in which better skills can be demonstrated. The lists printed below are not comprehensive, since other aspects will be identified each time the scripts are used. No list can ever be exhaustive because the nature of human interaction is that while there may be better ways of communicating, it is impossible to construct a set of ideals.

Examples of poor skills	*Examples of better skills*
not listening to various cues, signals	listening carefully, taking up issues
butting in, interrupting	allowing space, and some pauses
making assumptions, 'knowing' or assuming answers	seeking the individual's answers; extending the scope of the interview by offering possible links
trying to influence, or providing own solution, manipulative	shaping the interview, but encouraging the person to come to their own solution
asking leading or closed questions, and asking two questions at one time	asking open questions, questions which draw out more information, avoiding questions with yes/no answers
being threatening, heavy-handed, devaluing and defensive; officious, pressurizing, sarcastic and sexist	being friendly, gentle, sincere, encouraging, genuinely interested
showing lack of empathy, unable to acknowledge the true feelings	showing strong empathy and compassion
offering unrealistic promises/choices	offering realistic and rational assessment of genuine choices
speaking too much, too hurriedly, not allowing time for answers	slowing the pace down, especially when there are signs of panic; making space for each person to think

wandering away from painful material; changing the subject	helping painful material to be expressed and picking up difficult issues
being critical and shocked	being positive even if feeling surprised
being patronizing, talking down	not pretending to know when in fact doesn't know
being eager to get the information or outcome which the interviewer wants	clarifying issues, and alternative actions but ensuring choice is with the other
putting words into the other's mouth	using person's own words to reflect back, repeat, recap, and sum up
making the person out to be peculiar	showing how others might feel the same way
incongruous sharing of experience ('I get fed up too . . .')	using own experience without revealing it, to reach other's experience
inviting disloyalty to other people; running down (or defending too quickly) a third party	allowing different feelings to be expressed even if not agreeing; assuring confidentiality and discretion (where appropriate)
looking up information – not being well prepared	preparing information on person's background, where this may be helpful and known
not offering time to consider problems	offering further time for follow up, as well as time for reflection in the interview
getting angry when doesn't get own way	offering ongoing support, whatever the decision; defusing a crisis, and leaving door open

These two interviews probably contain most of what there is to know about good interviewing and about avoiding some very common mistakes. Anyone who can avoid half of what is in the left-hand column of the list above, and who can practise half of what is in the right-hand column, is well on the way to becoming a very caring and effective helper.

In order to develop these points, and to clarify them further, there are two sets of guidelines set out at the end of this chapter and examined one by one in the two following chapters. In every conversation there are times when we listen to the other, and times when we speak in response to what we have heard. The first set of guidelines is therefore about promoting better listening, and second set is about the skills that make for better responding. To categorize in this way these 'micro-skills', as they are often called, may appear contrived, or may make them seem artificial, and far from the manner in which ordinary conversations are held. In fact this is not so, since many good conversations, where people genuinely listen and talk to each other (as distinct from one-sided, boring conversations), naturally adopt ways of communicating that include these micro-skills.

The reason for identifying these skills is to assist learning, step by step, with the eventual aim that they become second nature, so permitting the *content* of any conversation or interview to become more important, without the *process* getting in the way. To begin with, learning new skills leads not unnaturally to a certain self-consciousness. The suggested exercises, which often contain an element of play, help to break that artificiality down. Each guideline emphasizes a different point, of which the interviewer will become aware when putting it into practice. Nevertheless it is important to remember that these micro-skills are a means to an end and not an end in themselves. They also demonstrate guidelines that are not necessarily comprehensive. It is easy to get the impression from books on social and communication skills that there are a limited number of rules to be followed to the letter, and that once they are followed everything else will fall into place. Good communication is much more subtle than that, including other features such as the attitude, the motivation and the manner of the interviewer.[2] I touch on these points in this book, but I cannot do so with the same effectiveness as you will get from the more personal feedback and interaction that the exercises and real life practice provide.

1. Guidelines for listening

1. Listen with undivided attention, without interrupting.
2. Remember what has been said, including the details (the more you listen and the less you say, the better your memory).
3. Listen to the 'bass line' – what is not openly said, but possibly is being felt.
4. Watch for body language, non-verbal clues that help you understand feelings.
5. Listen to yourself, how you might feel in a described situation, as a way of further understanding – this is the first step towards empathy.
6. Try to tolerate pauses and silences that are a little longer than is usual in conversations (and avoid asking lots of questions to break silences).
7. Create a comfortable and relaxed setting so that you can give attention to each other; keep calm even when you don't feel calm.

2. Guidelines for responding

8. Use words carefully; be as accurate as possible in describing feelings and ideas that you perceive (not just 'depressed' or 'angry').
9. Use your empathic understanding, again making this accurate, although also tentative (you may be wrong).
10. Keep questions to a minimum, unless:
    - you need precise information (in which case ask precise questions);
    - you want to open up an area (in which case use open-ended questions);
    - you wish to prompt (when rhetorical questions help). Avoid at all costs questions beginning 'Why . . . ?'
11. Use minimal prompts: 'Mm', 'Yes', or repeat the last few words.
12. Paraphrase or reflect accurately as:
    - a way of prompting;
    - an indication that you have been listening;
    - a way of checking out that you have heard correctly.
13. Avoid making judgements or loaded remarks.

14. Avoid changing the subject or interrupting unnecessarily.
15. Identify links between different experiences, events, reactions and ideas.
16. Avoid speaking too soon, too often, or for too long.

And finally, when you have responded:

17. Return to the listening mode, to watch and listen for the reaction to your response, as well as for anything new that emerges.

The following chapters describe these guidelines in more detail, and include exercises to enable you to practise the different skills.

TWO

Guidelines for Listening

1. Listen with undivided attention, without interrupting

It is so obvious, indeed almost insulting to a reader's intelligence, to observe that we have two ears and one mouth – but some helpers seldom use those senses in such a proportion, and instead react to people as if they had only one ear and two mouths. This guideline is clearly about the need to listen, but it is more than that – it is vital to listen well. The first step towards doing this is to practise listening with undivided attention.

This is easier said than done, largely because there is a great deal of external and internal 'noise' which can interfere with the task of listening intently. Some helpers have to conduct interviews in conditions that are far from ideal: the parish priest in a home full of distractions from television, children and other interruptions; the social worker in a partitioned office where noise from another interview room interferes; the line manager in a shared office or a noisy workplace. The complications of such external distractions are covered below, under Guideline 7.

But the other significant distraction takes place within the helper. When we recognize that, in the same length of time, we can absorb more when reading a text than when hearing a lecture, it is obvious that when we are listening to someone there is plenty of spare capacity in our mental processes. What happens to that spare capacity? So often the spare capacity is taken up with the listener's own thoughts and distractions. In expanding upon the ground rules, it will become clear that this spare capacity is best used by listening in additional ways, which includes listening to more than the obvious.

People who are trying to listen may therefore find it difficult to be fully attentive when preoccupied with their own agenda. The helper may have their own worries ('What am I meant to be doing next?'; even 'However am I going to deal with this situation?'), and this inevitably leads to some lack of concentration upon the person talking. The listener may find their thoughts triggered off by one of the speaker's remarks, and drift off into their own memories. One of the more advanced skills of listening is to be able to monitor these thoughts, but at this early stage they can be too distracting. The listener may be tired, and this is not helped if the speaker talks in a boring or monotonous way. The speaker may say things which irritate the listener, so that the listener gets caught up with their own feelings too strongly to pay real attention to what follows. The speaker may say things which predispose the listener to force the speaker into a stereotype, so that everything that is said thereafter is forced into a mould, and the listener fails to hear the individual. The speaker may describe situations or feelings which the listener is afraid of listening to, because of the sense of responsibility that comes from taking those issues further. There are even times when listeners fail to hear what is being said because they are not prepared to hear it. This last difficulty arises largely from semi-conscious or unconscious anxieties, and is difficult to overcome simply by trying to listen more intently: an openness to hearing things we do not want to hear comes from a level of maturity and self-acceptance which cannot be taught through this exercise.

It is important for the listener to pay attention, not simply to those things that may be embarrassing, difficult, painful, etc., but also to what at first seem insignificant little phrases and details. This exercise to practise listening, with both ears, is therefore in two parts: Exercise 2a below, which concentrates upon listening, and Exercise 2b in the next section (Guideline 2), which concentrates upon remembering the detail.

Exercise 2a

At this stage I want to encourage the reader simply to practise listening, without any need to respond. Therefore one of the rules of this part of the exercise is that the person listening is not allowed to say anything to the speaker. The only exception to this is a minimal response (as in Guideline 11) such as 'Mm', a nod of the head, or 'Yes'. The listener must not comment, nor ask any questions – always a temptation! In fact this rule should make it easier to listen, since one of the factors which interferes with good listening is concern about what we are going to say when the speaker has finished: 'Here's this man in front of me telling me about how angry he is with everyone; what on earth am I going to be able to say in reply?'

To start the exercise form pairs and identify an 'A' and a 'B' in each pair. A speaks to B for five minutes about his or her last week, or last holiday. Either topic should be described in as much detail as possible, including what may appear trivial details, but avoiding any incident or feeling which the speaker does not wish to divulge. There should be a timekeeper to keep an eye on the clock, to save the pairs worrying about time. When the first five minutes is over, time is called; and B now speaks to A about the same subject – either the last week, or the last holiday.

At the end of the second five minutes, discuss in the pairs what it felt like to speak without interruption – perhaps what it felt like if the speaker 'dried up' – and what it felt like to listen, having been told that there were to be no responses other than minimal ones. Some people find it easier to listen for the five minutes than they do to speak for that time. Others enjoy speaking, but find it difficult not to chip in with their own remarks while listening. Are you either of these types, or did you find both roles equally easy or equally difficult? What does that say about you as a person? It may be valuable to spend a little time reflecting upon this as well.

Having spent a few minutes talking over these different issues move on to the second part of this task (Exercise 2b).

2. Remember what has been said, including the details (the more you listen and the less you say, the better your memory)

Exercise 2b

Remain in the pairs formed in the first part of this exercise. B now plays back to A, as accurately as he or she can, all that A said in the first five minutes, in the order in which things were said and in as much detail as is possible. The person listening tries to emulate a tape-recorder. The rule now is that A is not permitted to prompt, though again may nod; and if B dries up, then A is not permitted to give assistance. Since this is a first attempt at remembering, some loss of memory is allowed for, so B need only play back for three minutes, not the full five! Once again a timekeeper watches the clock, and when the timekeeper announces the end of the first three minutes, A plays back to B what he or she heard in the second five minutes. At the end of this time, discuss in pairs how accurate each person's memory was, whether anything was omitted which felt important to the original speaker (and whether there might be any reason for this); and how it felt to hear what one said being played back (even though much of it was about fairly mundane matters). Was there any reason why some aspects of what was said were easier to remember than others?

The ability to memorize details obviously varies from person to person, to some extent depending upon how much their work involves them in the exercise of their memory. Memory can certainly be improved with constant practice – for example, evidence indicates that people who continue to exercise their minds as they age keep their brains more active. Generally, when listening to another in a helping situation, you can pick up a fairly obvious and often strong story line which provides a series of pegs to hang the details upon. In the above exercise the pegs may have been the days of the week – although the reason for asking for such ordinary topics to be spoken about (avoiding the dramatic) is to test out the capacity to remember the small details.

It is often the little things – the apparently innocuous remarks, the tiny phrases and the subtle emphasis – which enable the listener to hear more than the obvious (this is taken further in the next exercise). The substitution of 'but' for 'and' in a sentence, for example, may indicate hidden feelings. 'I went to hear my friend sing in a choir last week and I enjoyed it' does not have the same significance as, 'I went to hear my friend sing in a choir last week but I enjoyed it'. In the first statement there is little conclusion to be drawn from the use of 'and'. In the second version the conjunction 'but' appears to indicate that the speaker had reservations about going, but was pleasantly surprised to enjoy the concert. Other 'little things' which can be heard with careful listening include the infamous Freudian slip. A slip of the tongue may take a fraction of a second, and may be an innocuous substitution of one word for another; but some-times if someone says a word and then corrects it, the original word has some significance. A student was describing a gynaecological examination by a consultant, and his questions about former boyfriends. She said angrily, 'He was speaking to me as if I were the college whore, which I am'. She had not realized, and an inattentive listener might not have heard, that she had omitted the word 'not'.

In this instance one of her anxieties about sexual intimacy was indeed her association of sex with being immoral.

Careful listening enables different details mentioned by the speaker to be better remembered by the listener. These may include names of different people, particularly significant others, dates and other factual information. We have all experienced the warm glow when someone remembers our name or details about us, even though we may not have met for some time, when we would not have expected them to remember. Likewise we have all experienced a sense of disappointment or even frustration when someone does not remember an obviously important remark we have made a little earlier in a conversation. It is similarly rewarding for the listener, who has remembered some detail from a previous meeting and included this in a conversation, when the other person says, 'Fancy you remembering that!'; and if the listener feels pleased, this is only a measure of how pleased the other person must feel that they have mattered sufficiently for such personal information to be remembered.

Those whose task it is to listen professionally may think that they should take notes of conversations, in order to remember these details. Those whose working day includes many interviews (of whatever nature) clearly need to record some details, not only for an agency's records, but (even when the helper works on his or her own) as an *aide-mémoire* for the next time they meet the person. Long-term memory can often be aided by making notes, even when they are not directly referred to. It is in fact surprising how much can be retained, sometimes triggered off in the memory by a chance remark in a subsequent meeting. Nevertheless, even when memories are clear, it is good practice for those who conduct regular interviews to refresh their minds from time to time on the progress of the work. Some information can be forgotten, and such a regular review can assist the helper in bringing a series of interviews back to what is central.

Remembering is therefore made easier by taking notes. In some interviews it may be necessary to make notes at the time: a doctor finds this saves time in the context of a busy surgery; the social worker may need to record precise factual information to assist a material request; the pastor may need to record biographical and personal details when arranging a wedding or a baptism. In these circumstances note-taking is normal, and is accepted as routine by the person who has come to ask for assistance.

Yet note-taking when personal and emotional difficulties are being expressed can be very off-putting. It may seem as if intimate details are being written down (almost like taking evidence); it makes the interview too formal (even if any interview inevitably has elements of formality built into it); it is very difficult for a listener to record notes and at the same time to look at the speaker (Guideline 4 will demonstrate how essential it is to be able to do this). Where conversations are much more personal, and do not involve the necessity of getting factual information crystal clear, it is far better to record any notes after the interview or conversation is over. Some helpers like to make notes immediately afterwards; others like to let the conversation percolate within them before putting their thoughts on paper. Such notes are highly personal, and not intended for anyone else to see; they may reveal as much about the helper's inner responses as they do about the speaker's outward content. They need to be kept very secure so that they are not seen by anyone else, and safely destroyed when they are no longer needed. Exercise 17 demonstrates one way of recording an interview.

Exercises 2a and 2b are helpful in promoting short-term recall to use in any post-interview record. Short-term memory is important, and the listener simply has to hold details and factual material long enough in memory to record them later. Given practice, not only in memorizing but also in recording, the helper will find that it is possible to remember more than half of an interview – even an hour's meeting – and to recall many of the detailed remarks which were made and seemed to have some significance. Interviews in which listening plays a crucial part often take the form of the person seeking help speaking for a number of minutes, followed by the listener responding briefly, and this leading to another period when the speaker continues the story. Memory is improved by recalling what has been said in these different sections of the conversation. As long as the listener is able to respond appropriately (see Chapter 3), actually taking up what the speaker has been saying, and not going off on their own tangent, an interview frequently progresses from one peg to another, making overall recall at the end rather simpler.

Remembering, like listening, becomes more difficult if the listener speaks too often or for too long (see Guideline 16). By keeping quiet, and listening carefully, it is possible to remember more. Remembering is also difficult if the listener is too anxious, perhaps wondering all the time what to say or do next. An interviewer who is concerned for himself or herself, worrying about how effective he or she is being, will often have trouble in recalling more than a few of the most obvious remarks that the speaker has made.

These first two guidelines are intimately linked. The more attention the listener pays to the speaker, and the less to the external or internal distractions, the greater is the possibility of remembering what transpired. We know from our everyday experience that those occasions when we fail to remember something we have been told or asked to do are the times when, for one reason or another, we have not been fully listening.

If that were all there is to listening, it would be a fairly easy task, as long as we could maintain this particular frame of mind. Unfortunately there is yet much more to consider, all of which increases the effectiveness of an interview, and which in itself imposes another, equally legitimate agenda for the listener to think about. Bearing in mind that listening attentively and remembering accurately become more complicated as the other guidelines are added, this is the point when other ways of listening, which will themselves assist the task of responding, need to be added to the basic skills.

3. Listen to the 'bass line' – what is not openly said, but possibly is being felt

What makes a good piece of music? This is a major question which musicians, psychologists and philosophers of aesthetics may wish to argue about. I ask it here simply to draw a parallel between my observation about what music I like to hear and another aspect of listening. For me a piece of music is enjoyable to hear time and again when it has much more to it than a good melody line. The first time we hear a piece of music we probably hear the melody; subsequent hearings make us listen to other features – the left hand as well as the right hand on the piano, or the scoring of other instruments in an orchestra or band than those that have the melody line. Whether or not a musicologist would agree with me, much of the pleasure of repeated listening comes in picking up another melody, or an underlying rhythm, a counterpoint, or a variation – as in a fugue.

When a person speaks, particularly about emotional matters, there is often a main melody, but also a bass line. There is a major theme, a story line, perhaps one clear emotional response, all of which are fairly obvious. Yet there are often other thoughts and feelings present, especially when the story is charged with feeling. Consider the following situations.

1. Annette is describing how ill her aged mother is, and that the amount of suffering her mother is going through will make death a merciful release. If we begin to look for a bass line, we see first an ambiguity in the term 'merciful release': for whom – Annette or her mother? If Annette tends to concentrate on her mother, in listening we might also hear how she is describing her own reactions too. While the dominant feeling she is talking about is one of relief, we might also expect there to be other underlying feelings of sadness, or even guilt at having such thoughts about release.

2. Brian is talking about his discontent with his son's school, and the poor education he feels his son is receiving. Beneath his angry tones (whether or not Brian is justified in thinking this) there is probably also some anxiety about this young man's future. There may be elements of the pressure Brian feels for his son to succeed, coming from his own experiences at school.

3. Carol wishes to talk through a personal dilemma. Her boyfriend is pressing her to have a full sexual relationship, and she is not at all sure that this is right for her. She talks somewhat disparagingly about her other friends, and how easily they slip into sexual relationships. But could Carol also be somewhat envious of her friends' ability to enter relationships without appearing to think twice about it? Or is she thinking, looking at them, that she should go along with what they are doing rather than stay with her own values? Is she wondering what all this is doing to her relationship? What Carol describes therefore has a number of different elements.

It is often because of these conflicting emotions, contradictory feelings and opposing sets of values that people need someone to talk to. If their feelings are straightforward, they can usually manage them, even when what they are experiencing is painful. Grief, for example, is very natural and, though it can be exceedingly painful, it is not necessarily a problem needing the help of an outsider. Friends and relatives usually provide the kind of support and attention which makes the passage through grief tolerable. But where grief is compounded with other strong feelings, such as anger or guilt, conflicts often arise, and such contradictory feelings (including the less acceptable feelings and thoughts) cannot always be so readily expressed to relatives and friends, or even to oneself. Because conflicting feelings tend to cause difficulties, it is important for a helper to listen to what is being said at different levels, so that less acceptable, less easily expressed emotions and thoughts can be brought into the open, in addition to the obvious feelings.

Exercise 3

This exercise is a little more demanding than the last, perhaps more so for the speaker than for the listener. The task of the listener is similar to that in Exercise 2 – that is, to say nothing except perhaps give a few minimal prompts, until the speaker has finished their story. (This will take a few minutes, but probably not as many as the five minutes in Exercise 2.) The speaker is given a story to tell which involves playing a character talking about a situation, in which there is one very obvious feeling on the surface. The story contains the possibility of other thoughts and feelings, some of which are listed after the story lines below. Other thoughts and feelings may become apparent in the way each participant plays the role. The people telling the story should remember one important point – that they should concentrate on expressing the obvious emotion in the words they use: all the other feelings are implied in the way the story is told, and so may come through in the tone of voice, facial expression and gestures, or from the listener reading between the lines.

When the speaker has finished his or her story, the listener should identify first the obvious emotion, which has been expressed verbally, and then draw out the other feelings and thoughts which were implicit, checking out with the speaker whether these were indeed present, or were possibly present despite the speaker not fully realizing it. So, for example, taking the situations listed above, the listener might say to Annette: 'The obvious feeling is the wish for relief and release', but the bass-line feelings might be 'relief for yourself as well as your mother, sadness at the thought of losing her, and some guilty feelings about wishing her to die'. To Brian the listener could say, 'You are obviously angry at the education your son is getting, but you also look worried, and I wonder whether you are wanting to put pressure on your son as well as the school'. To Carol the listener might say, 'You are obviously in a dilemma: perhaps you are also worried lest you lose your boyfriend; you might feel envious of the ease with which your friends make such decisions; perhaps there's even an aspect of you which would like a more intimate relationship'. None of these statements are precisely the same as the response the helper would give to the speaker in a real situation. The exercise is primarily about listening for the bass line; how the bass-line feelings are reflected back to the speaker is considered in the next chapter, on guidelines for responding.

To engage in this exercise, form pairs and take it in turns to be the speaker and the listener, selecting from the stories below one that is appropriate for you, again without choosing one that is actually a personal issue for you. The possible bass-line feelings, which you try to express in any way other than the actual words you use, are listed in square brackets at the end of each story.

1. Imagine that you have been left some money, and you now have a wonderful opportunity to visit your eldest brother, who has been asking you for years to come and see him and his family in Australia. You have not met for years, and have never seen his wife or children. But he left England under a cloud after a series of rows with your parents, and you feel he was very stupid in some of the things he said and did. So although you have always looked up to him, and are looking forward to the reunion, you are also aware that old family wounds may be reopened. As you tell this story, stress in the words you use the obvious emotion, which is excitement at this opportunity of visiting him in Australia. Try to avoid using emotive words to describe anything else in the story line, and see what your partner draws out from the situation. [Possible bass-line emotions and thoughts in this situation: anxiety, resentment, anger, fear.]

2. Imagine that you are a teacher who is waiting for a piece of work from a student, who keeps coming to you with a series of very plausible excuses, all of which make you feel sorry for him or concerned about him. First he left the project outline on the school bus; then his parents were ill and he had to look after them; then he couldn't find any of the books in the library; then his notes got thrown away by accident; and finally he says he has

had his bag stolen with the finished project in it. He is always upset by each misfortune. As you tell this story, stress in the words you use the obvious emotion, which is care, concern or sympathy. Try to avoid emotive words to describe anything else in the story line, and see what your partner draws out from the situation. [Possible bass-line emotions and thoughts in this situation: frustration, anger, helplessness, irritation.]

3. Imagine that you are thrilled to have found a cottage to retire to. It is by the sea, in a quiet hamlet with fewer than 100 people, no pub, no church – just a sleepy unspoiled place. And how different this will be from the last 30 years, living in such a large city, so busy at work and with the church, and all your friends – you may elaborate on all the things you have done. As you tell this story, stress in the words you use the obvious emotion, which is how thrilled you are. Try to avoid emotive words to describe anything else in the story line, and see what your partner draws out of the situation. [Possible bass-line emotions and thoughts in this situation: anxiety at going somewhere new, making new friends; loss of present friends and opportunities; coping with relative isolation.]

4. Imagine that you are very hurt because you have been in the church choir for 30 years, and the vicar has now told you that he thinks older people should retire gracefully and make way for younger voices. He did not say it, but implied that your voice was wobbly; it was so hurtful of him to remind you of your age. You feel so miserable. You don't feel like going to his church any more. You were nearly in tears when he told you. You dropped things all evening when you got home and smashed one of your finest plates. How can a man of God say such hurtful things? As you tell this story stress in the words you use the obvious emotion, which is being so hurt. Try to avoid emotive words to describe anything else in the story line, and see what your partner draws out of the situation. [Possible bass-line emotions and thoughts in this situation: anger; difficulty expressing anger as a Christian; feeling 'past it'.]

5. Imagine you are apologizing to your immediate superior at work. Everything has gone wrong with an assignment. Your

eldest daughter came in very late last evening, and in waiting up for her you became so tired you forgot to set your alarm for an earlier time. So you woke this morning with only half an hour to spare to catch the train to see your potential client. The car needed petrol and there was a long queue at the garage, the traffic was terrible, and you had a long wait at the booking office. Even though your train was itself late, you missed it by half a minute – it was drawing out as you ran on to the platform. The next train was due ten minutes later but was delayed by a points failure, so you got into your destination an hour late and missed your appointment with the representative of another firm; he had left his office with a message saying the deal was off. As you tell this story, stress in the words you use the obvious emotion, which is how sorry you are. Try to avoid emotive words to describe anything else in the story line, and see what your partner draws out of the situation. [Possible bass-line emotions and thoughts in this situation: worry about your daughter being late; frustration; anger; fear of losing job.]

6. Imagine you are complaining to your section head, because you are very angry with the new foreman. You've always been a hard-working, reliable employee, and you've never missed a day through illness. Recently a rush job came into your department, but unfortunately your wife and child went down with a nasty bug, and you had to stay at home to get the doctor in, look after them, etc. Your new foreman greeted you the next day by accusing you of being lazy, of letting them down, etc. It is the last straw: he is always making snide comments, picking on you – and after all you have done for the firm! As you tell this story, stress in the words you use the obvious emotion, which is how angry you are. Try to avoid emotive words to describe anything else in the story line, and see what your partner draws out of the situation. [Possible bass-line emotions and thoughts in this situation: feeling hurt; wanting to get your own back; worry about what your immediate superior might think of your absence.]

When each partner has told their story, and each has had the chance to draw out the bass-line feelings and thoughts, discuss how the listener arrived at his or her conclusions. Were there any non-verbal clues, such as a clenched fist, or a furrowed brow? Was the speaker's tone of voice hinting at other feelings, such as an exciting story being told in a flat way? Did the listener so enter into the situation described that they could imagine what other feelings might have been present? Were there any other pointers? The way in which we detect these other feelings and thoughts (thoughts can be just as important as the traditional counselling emphasis upon feelings) is the central concern of Guidelines 4 and 5.

4. Watch for body language, non-verbal clues that help you understand feelings

Exercise 4

Before reading the description of this guideline, and the exercises that follow, list what you feel might be the ten most basic emotions which we experience. (Note: emotions are moods, not needs: e.g. envy is an emotion, hunger is a need.) If you are working in small groups, try to agree upon which ten emotions could be included in a joint list. At this stage, concentrate on identifying the major clusters of feeling (so, for example, hatred, irritation and perhaps even frustration could all be lumped together under the one basic emotion of anger); later we shall consider the variations in mood, and the different synonyms that can be used to describe various levels of emotion.

Feelings are very important. To suppress them, for whatever reason (such as fear of losing control, or fear of someone else's criticism), makes a person uncomfortable or even distressed, and makes it much more difficult for someone to make choices and decisions, or to carry out commonplace tasks. Conversely, the opportunity to express feelings – particularly to express in a safe setting feelings which are normally felt to be unacceptable – provides relief and release, and can for the time being at least help to reduce them and enable a person to think and act more clearly. It is not just feelings that get suppressed and hidden; unwelcome thoughts do too – although non-verbal communication tends to hint more at feelings than it does at thoughts. Unwelcome thoughts, together with unwelcome feelings, are more usually identified through listening to yourself, as in Guideline 5.

Non-verbal signs are the very first communications we receive from a person seeking an interview or asking for help. Before people open their mouths, they sometimes show through non-verbal behaviour and expression how they feel – perhaps how they are feeling about the interview which is about to take place, or perhaps about the general situation which brings them. The listener is also someone who watches, and so might spot this basic mood at the point of meeting a person – whether in a waiting room, or as they enter the room, or even when the person opens their own front door. Non-verbal clues continue to be observable as people walk into the room, both in the way in which they cross the room and sit down on the chair, as well as in their sitting position. This is, of course, only the initial way in which a listener can learn from non-verbal communication; it may be very important to the start of an interview, especially if a person looks anxious. The listener's first task is often to help the speaker to feel more at ease. This might be done through a reflection upon direct observation ('You look rather nervous about seeing me'); or less directly by attempting to smooth the way with a gentle introduction, explanation of the meeting, or even with pleasantries.

This next exercise specifically looks at the start of an interview and at the way in which the listener can pick up clues in the opening moments, before a word has been spoken.

Exercise 5

In groups of five or six (or this could be done with smaller numbers taking several turns), sit in a circle with one empty chair. Each person leaves the group in turn, and where possible goes out of a door. While this person is away from the group he or she decides which of the basic emotions (listed in Exercise 4) to try and portray *non-verbally*, for the group to guess. The person now knocks at the door, and enters the room, walks across to the group, and sits in the empty chair, all the time trying to express non-verbally how he or she feels with that emotion dominant. The person remains silent (but still tries to convey how they are feeling) until the group guesses, or gets near enough. This exercise takes only a short time: but it provides opportunities for recognizing what might be presented in the initial contact between listener and future speaker.

Non-verbal communication is present throughout any interaction. Facial expression, hand gestures and bodily posture frequently reflect what is being described verbally. There are also instances when the person speaking is very flat in their delivery, but provides clues to feelings through non-verbal signs; or where the speaker is describing (or denying) one feeling, and yet expressing non-verbally the opposite feeling, or different feelings. Someone may clench his fist tightly and say 'I'm not angry', while appearing to be feeling angry, yet being either unaware of it, or afraid to admit it. The person who says they are very angry but who is obviously shaking may be expressing not only their rage, but also showing that the anger is a response to fear.

Facial expression is also a powerful, if silent, 'voice'. With the exception of the truly poker-faced, most of us cannot help giving away our feelings through automatic muscular reaction to a situation. It is probably true that, like many species of animals, we too recognize these non-verbal communications at a subliminal level and react to them, again often automatically. In our homes, among people we know well, we allude to non-verbal communication naturally: 'You're looking very cross; what's biting you? That was a big sigh.' In the helping interview it is therefore possible to make much more of non-verbal communication, firstly by becoming more conscious of it, and secondly, when it feels appropriate, by describing it verbally.

Exercise 6

This exercise is called 'Silent Movies',[1] and can be worked on by using a video or in the following interpersonal way. One person speaks as if with the sound turned down – in other words, mouthing the words but not letting a sound leave the larynx. It is important that the 'speaker' tells an ordinary story, allowing facial or hand expression to come naturally. Exaggerated facial expression or miming with the hands are not only unnecessary but will detract from the point of the exercise, which is that there are obvious clues to what a person is feeling, even in the most ordinary forms of speaking.

Form pairs as in earlier exercises (although where the group is large enough, make these different pairings). Each partner is given a list of four situations, from the list below, and each in turn gives a short account of each situation (silently), until all eight have been gone through. Each situation is spoken but no words are actually uttered. As the partner finishes speaking, the listener is asked to guess not what the story was about (that is only a vehicle), but what emotion was being conveyed in the story through the non-verbal expressions. Since the room is normally quiet for this exercise (except perhaps for some laughter), the guesses might have to be whispered, so that other pairs do not overhear answers to situations which they have yet to come to. At the end of the exercise both partners should try and identify what expressions, particularly facial ones, provided clues to the dominant feeling.

1. Tell a story of riding on a bus, when a group of drunken youths got on and tried to cause trouble; and how *frightened* you were.

2. Tell a story of visiting a town where you used to live and how *surprised* you were at the many new buildings, roads, etc., which had sprung up since you were last there.

3. Tell a story about eating in a works canteen and being *disgusted* by the manners of the man sitting opposite you.

4. Tell a story of how *angry* you were when you discovered how badly your car had been serviced.

5. Tell a story of how *pleased* you are with the new house you have just bought.

6. Tell a story of how *sad* you felt when you heard that your friend's marriage had broken up.

7. Tell a story about how *envious* you feel of your neighbours, who are always having new things delivered to their home.

8. Tell a story of feeling *excited* by the dishy and sexy new person (man or woman) who has just joined the office staff.

Compare the observations that each pair has made, and contrast the cues and the subtle differences. There is a difference, for example, between fear and surprise because although in both cases eyebrows tend to be raised and the eyes open wider, yet the mouth position is different. There is also a difference between pleasure and sexual excitement, seen in the difference between a smile and a leer. In the latter case eyebrows go up and down, and there may even be a sideways glance. Some feelings have very distinctive reactions (the wrinkling of the nose in disgust, and – although less visually obvious – the tightening of the throat). It may also be worthwhile watching for facial expressions in a mirror, if this does not make participants feel too self-conscious!

To summarize: not only do we have two ears (one of which might be said to listen to the obvious details as a way of remembering, and the other to bass-line emotions and thoughts), but we also have two eyes, with which to watch for the non-verbal clues to understanding the speaker. By listening and observing carefully, the listener builds up a fuller picture of the speaker, and is in a more informed position to voice some of those observations when the right time comes.

Exercise 7

With sharpened sensitivity to non-verbal communication, especially to facial expressions, you can now develop responses to non-verbal reactions in the other person – as in this exercise. Imagine, for instance, that you are asking someone to do a favour for you, or requesting a member of your staff to undertake an extra task. The interaction, both in words and non-verbal response, might go as follows:

YOURSELF   I wonder whether you could do such-and-such for me?
         [The other person looks concerned]
YOURSELF   You seem concerned at my suggestion. Is there some difficulty about that?
         [The other person explains that he or she is rather worried, but perhaps then (having had the feeling acknowledged) goes on to accept the request]

For this exercise, stay in the pairings formed in Exercise 6. Each in turn plays the person in the role of carer, and the other a person who has come to talk. Imagine the conversation is at a point when it must be drawn to a close. The carer (i.e. the listener) asks whether the speaker wishes to come and talk some more next week. The speaker responds non-verbally to this suggestion. The carer tries to pick up the response which flashes across the other's face, and reflects what he or she sees. For example:

HELPER   Perhaps you'd like to come and talk again next week?
        [Speaker looks shocked]
HELPER   You seem surprised at my suggestion.

The two partners are provided with two different sets of non-verbal responses, which are used in reaction to the phrase each time it is spoken ('Perhaps you'd like to come and talk again next week?'). After observing the response, the listener puts in his or her own words what has been observed. It may be wise to leave a slight pause to consider how best to express the observation.

Partner A: Respond to the listener's invitation to come and talk again next week by showing, non-verbally, the following reactions (one each time you repeat the exercise, taking it in turns to be listener and speaker):
1. express worry or concern at the suggestion;
2. express relief that the suggestion has been made;
3. express surprise that the suggestion has been made.

Partner B: Respond to the listener's invitation to come and talk again next week by showing, non-verbally, the following reactions (one each time you repeat the exercise, taking it in turns to be listener and speaker):
1. express sadness at the suggestion, which means stopping for now;
2. express uncertainty at the suggestion;
3. express enthusiasm for the suggestion.

The group members can discuss their attempts to find the right words in responding to non-verbal communication, perhaps looking at the subtlety of language.

5. Listen to yourself, how you might feel in a described situation, as a way of further understanding – this is the first step towards empathy

Had we three ears, this guideline might require the third to be tuned in yet another direction. We can speak of an 'inner ear', one that is tuned to our own feelings, thoughts and reactions – it is this that the guideline addresses. One of the characteristics of good listeners is their ability to use themselves – but not (as it sometimes appears in counselling literature) by openly disclosing details of their own personal lives. (This point will be taken up later in Guideline 13.) A much more effective way of using yourself is to monitor both the effect of the speaker on you (because that may provide some clues as to how that person makes others feel),[2] and also to listen to your own feelings and ideas about the speaker's situation.

Put another way, it is possible to imagine how it would feel to be in the speaker's position: 'If I were in trouble with the law, how would I feel?' 'If my father had walked out on my mother, how would I feel?' 'If my child was very ill in hospital, how would I feel?' The feelings that come to mind might be more extensive and varied than the one feeling which is perhaps being expressed by the speaker. Some of the thoughts and reactions which we ourselves might experience will possibly not be among those which the speaker is experiencing, but some may help us to make an empathic response.

Imagining how we might feel in a certain situation is not in itself empathy, but it is the first step towards empathy. Empathy really begins when we can leave behind what we ourselves might feel or think, and move into what the speaker might be feeling or thinking. There may be dimensions to the speaker's situation which have little or nothing in common with our own. For example, Jack and Jill are spending more than they can afford from their unemployment benefit on drinking with friends in the evenings. The carer, who is comfortably cushioned from unemployment, might imagine that if he were in their situation he would cut down on the number of times he went out in order to save enough money to pay the bills – whereas Jack and Jill are getting into debt. 'But', says the unthinking carer, 'haven't you thought of going out less?' The complete lack of empathy shown in this remark becomes obvious when Jill quickly retorts, 'When you are unemployed and there is nothing to do all day, you need to go out in the evenings'. At this point the carer realizes that this is a dimension of their experience which he does not appreciate and cannot fully understand, and he may realize that the solution is not as simple as he had first thought. Had he tried to imagine it, he might have responded more appropriately.

Empathy should not be confused with sympathy. The listener may or may not feel sympathetic towards the speaker. If the listener feels too sympathetic, or indeed is too caught up in sharing the same emotional response, it may be difficult for the listener to be sufficiently objective to go on listening well, or to look for dimensions other than the obvious. Similarly, the listener can be empathic without feeling much sympathy. In the example above, the carer may not feel much sympathy towards Jack and Jill for spending too much on going out and then being in debt; on the other hand he may feel sympathetic towards them because they are unemployed and have to live on such low income. Only if the listener is empathic to their being unemployed is it possible for him to imagine how their spending money on going out can be an attempt to make life tolerable. Then it is possible to be empathic to their being in debt. Furthermore, even where sympathy is readily felt, an empathic response is in most cases much more helpful than a sympathetic response, however well meant (as we see under Guideline 13).

Empathy starts with listening to yourself ('What would I feel in that situation?') and may involve finding out more information, which then enables the question to be asked silently, 'What is this other person feeling in their situation?' If the listener has actually been in that situation, it may seem as if their empathy will be accurate. This may be true, but it is an incautious assumption because no two situations are ever identical. What has led up to a situation, the complexities of the present experience and all the possible permutations make empathy from our own experience difficult to get right. The empathic response, as long as it is accurate, can be extraordinarily effective – although where it is not, it can create a feeling of not being heard. The accuracy of an empathic response is therefore dependent upon careful listening, through delicate exploration of the issues and feelings, and through listening to yourself.

At this stage it is enough to spell out the ground rule, 'Listen to yourself'. In a later section (Guideline 9) I look at ways of turning this into an empathic response. Here I suggest an exercise which is more in the nature of a party game, but which starts you on the process of listening to yourself, and of responding to others from imagining what it may be like to be in their situation. (Another exercise in making *accurate* empathic responses is found in Chapter 3, under Guideline 9.)

Exercise 8

This exercise can be used in two different ways. The first and most straightforward method is to take some of the statements in the list of situations set out below, and to discuss what empathic responses might be made to someone who is in those situations.

The second method uses the list below for a variation on the party game in which guests have to guess the name of the character pinned on their back. This method works best when there are more than eight or nine people in the group. Use name cards, with a situation written on each. Start by giving a card and a blank sheet of paper to each member of the group. Each person pins the card to another's back (without that person first seeing it), and they all then mingle as they would at a party.

As two people meet they each take a look at the card on the other's back, and then each makes an empathic response to the other, such as 'You might be feeling worried', or 'That sounds a difficult situation to be in'. Each records the response given to them, so that on their paper they build up a list of responses to the situation pinned to their back. Once the empathic response has been given, each person is permitted to narrow down the situation by asking the other person one question, which must be capable of being answered 'Yes' or 'No', such as, 'Is this something to do with my family?', or 'Does it concern money?'

The two people then move off and find others to respond to, to receive a response from, and to ask and answer one question. As the game proceeds each person first shows their existing list of responses to the other, so that a new empathic response can be made, and with these varied responses the questioner is gaining a more accurate picture. If the responder sees that someone has already been told that they might be worried, they need to say something new, such as, 'That might put a strain on your relationship'. This may seem a hard task, but experience of this game has shown that good empathic responses, together with the information coming from the questions, enables at least half the people to guess their own situation after six to eight encounters around the room. It helps participants realize much about making good empathic responses, which they tend to give in order to help each other to get their situations right.

It is important to bear in mind throughout the exercise that empathy is not sympathy, nor is it about giving advice. This may need stressing before starting either method of using this exercise. Otherwise the most common response tends to be, 'If I were you, I'd . . .' (advice-giving), or 'I *am* sorry . . .' (sympathy).

Situations for practising empathic responses

What empathic responses might be made to the following situations?

1. We have heard that we have been accepted as adoptive parents of a physically handicapped child.
2. A lorry ran into our new car when it was parked, causing a lot of damage to it.
3. I went to a party last night and drank so much I don't remember what I said or did in the last part of the evening.
4. We have just been left £5000 in a will. My partner wants to spend it on the holiday of a lifetime. I want to spend it on improving our home.
5. I have offended my mother-in-law, but don't know what it is I am supposed to have done.
6. The neighbours are objecting to planning permission for a much-needed extension to our house.
7. We were going out for a meal last night to an expensive restaurant, but our youngest was ill, and we had to cancel it.
8. My partner has just accepted an invitation for us to go to dinner with a couple whom she/he knows I don't like.
9. My brother and his wife have just bought a lovely place on the coast as a holiday cottage.
10. I've been invited to make an important speech welcoming foreign visitors to our town.
11. I have to decide whether to leave my job and apply for another, which will mean moving, or to stay with the present firm which may go bust.
12. My daughter is heartbroken at the break up of her first 'real' relationship, though I wasn't sure about the boy.
13. I have been accepted as a mature student at a local university, which means I can study as well as look after the children.
14. My son has been suspended from school for vandalism but he tells me he had no part in it.
15. I have just heard that the travel company with whom we booked our first Continental holiday has gone into liquidation.
16. My partner and I are going on our first holiday without the children since the first was born 18 years ago.
17. I am waiting for the purchaser of our house to sell his before we can exchange contracts on a superb house that we fear we might lose.
18. It is the anniversary of my previous marriage – 25 years ago today. My former partner has sent a friendly note.

19. I have recently learned that a growth which the doctors at first thought might be malignant is in fact harmless.
20. My daughter wants to go on an educational cruise because all her friends are going, but we can't afford it.
21. I have an interview for a job next week – although I have been short-listed 20 times so far and haven't got anywhere.
22. My partner gets a lot out of involvement in the local church, although I have no interest in religion.
23. I have been expecting promotion, but have just made a stupid mistake over my work which jeopardizes my chances.
24. I have just given up smoking.
25. My life is a blank.

After the exercise, discuss the difficulties of making accurate empathic responses.

6. Try to tolerate pauses and silences that are a little longer than is usual in conversations

As you begin to appreciate these guidelines – learning to listen, not interrupting, listening to yourself, and using observation of non-verbal signs – the speaker is given the chance to be more fully heard. But what then do we say as the person seeking help finishes their story? Most helpers long for the opportunity to show how useful they can be, and as soon as there is a break, in they go with their response. A few even have the irritating habit of interrupting or finishing sentences without waiting to see what the other really wants to say.

Has the speaker finished? There may be a pause – but what sort of pause is it? Perhaps the speaker is only stopping to take breath, or more likely to take stock. Perhaps he or she wishes to say something more. Perhaps the speaker knows what they want to say but cannot yet find the right words. Perhaps the speaker has come to an embarrassing part of the story, where a pause is necessary to summon up the courage to go on. Or perhaps the speaker is at this point waiting for the listener to reply. These are all possibilities.

Perhaps the carer has just finished responding, and the speaker says nothing. During this pause it is not necessary for the carer to say any more. Instead there is an opportunity for the carer to watch the speaker's reactions, to see whether what the carer just said has made the other person silent because the carer has not understood;

or because they wish to reflect upon the words before replying; or whether what has been said has caused some anxiety. Similarly, if the carer asks a question, the person to whom it is addressed probably needs a little time to consider the reply – either to find the right words or to think about the answer.

It has been noticed that teachers tend to allow only a short time (0.7 seconds on average) for their students to answer questions addressed to them, and as a result only the quickest students answer in that time; other children, who know the answer but need a little more time to frame it, are passed over in favour of the eager ones who put up their hands quickly. When teachers are trained to leave just a couple of seconds before moving on to another student, the response rate in the class, and the level of participation, shoot up. In interviewing too, if a question is not answered immediately, the interviewer is tempted to frame a second question, perhaps in an effort to help; but in fact this is normally very confusing, because the person now has two questions to think about instead of one.

In suggesting the need to allow a longer silence than we often permit in a conversation, I am certainly not advocating long silences such as can occur in counselling or psychotherapy with clients who have become accustomed to periods of reflection. Such silences seem longer than they are, and so they can be used effectively only when both parties are accustomed to them. In counselling, clients learn the value of silence. In the more ordinary interviews, when the listener is using counselling skills without offering formal counselling, the guideline urges the listener to wait just that little longer than is customary in conversation, to see if there is more that the speaker wishes to say.

Although the following example comes from a counselling session, it makes a valuable point. Lenny had been coming for several weeks when, on one occasion, he started the session by saying, 'I don't think there's anything to talk about today'. I began to think back to the previous meeting, but because I was trying to remember what had been said then, a silence naturally followed. On this occasion I had not had time to refresh my memory, and so my thought processes took longer than usual. The silence lasted for a minute or so. I was still racking my brain when Lenny broke the silence: 'Well, actually there is something I could say, but I'm not sure I want to mention it'. His remark gave me the opportunity to take up his hesitation, and the session proceeded with some new and important information that Lenny had not shared previously. What would have happened to that information had I been in a better position to remember what had transpired the previous week? I might have been tempted to ask about a matter raised then ('I wonder how such and such is going . . . ?'). As it was, the silence forced on us by my inability to remember led to a significant breakthrough of new material.

In Chapter 4 there is an exercise in which all the guidelines are put together. There is a tendency (as Chapter 3 shows) for those listening to ask too many questions, but sometimes the listener runs out of questions, and a somewhat embarrassing silence falls. On these occasions it is often the person who is trying to tell their story who breaks the silence, perhaps introducing another feature of the story which the listener would probably have not picked up by asking a question. Such occurrences demonstrate the value of the listener deliberately allowing the speaker enough time to talk about a different issue, or to expand on something they have already mentioned, rather than filling the time and imposing the agenda. (An exercise which incorporates some practice of silence is included in Chapter 3.)

7. Create a comfortable and relaxed setting

The psychoanalyst D. W. Winnicott once commended his own list of guidelines to social workers, concluding with the words: 'You are not frightened, nor do you become overcome with guilt-feelings when your client goes mad, disintegrates, runs out in the street in a night-dress, attempts suicide and perhaps succeeds'.[3] The title of the book in which this paper appears includes the phrase 'the facilitating environment', which clearly has some relevance in any helping context. My guidelines are concerned to promote facilitating skills which the helper can use in interviews and conversations.

When Winnicott writes of the facilitating environment, he refers not so much to a place or to physical surroundings as to the carer, because it is through their personal qualities that this facilitating can be offered. Those who care for others – from parents through to professionals – need to be both caring and careful, as well as supportive, containing, able to hold anxiety and to maintain an unshocked and unshockable demeanour. Winnicott's words may appear to relate more to the extreme instances of distress that can

occur to anyone who comes for help, and therefore the helper too –
but what he writes applies equally well to the less extreme situations
which are part of the work of every helper.

There are some disturbing situations in which a carer needs to
know when and how to refer the client, or the person seeking help,
to more appropriate resources (see Chapter 6). There are many
other rather more ordinary situations in which people can get very
upset, or angry, or argumentative – and in these situations as well,
the helper tries to stay calm. It is important to remember that a
helper may not *feel* calm, and *may* be shocked, or may feel personally upset. It is a fallacy and a fantasy to imagine that highly skilled
and experienced carers can approach any situation with equanimi-
ty. They too feel thrown. Indeed it might even be said that people
can only effectively help if they are moved to feeling by the situation, as much as a beginner would be. The real difference between
experienced and inexperienced helpers in these situations is that the
former have learned that generally a calm and accepting response
nearly always helps the situation, and provides the space in which to
consider the best intervention to make.

No helper is, or should be, immune to feelings of panic, guilt,
hurt, helplessness or anger. The important point is not to let such
feelings show. While the tongue can be bridled, the helper needs to
be equally careful not to show negative responses non-verbally.
Being poker-faced, at least in relation to adverse reactions, is a useful attribute to develop. I have indicated already how easy it is to
give away one's feelings by non-verbal signs – and it is as easy for the
listener to do as for the speaker. Feelings can be shown by raised eyebrows or a frown, or by body posture. The helper's folded arms may
mask tension, or represent a barrier against the speaker. Leaning
forward in the chair may appear to indicate interest, but is often
experienced by the other as threatening. The non-verbal message of
calm is better conveyed by keeping still, moving slowly, and main-
taining an interested and even expression.

Although this guideline principally addresses the manner of the
helper, the physical setting of the interview also has a part to play.
The setting depends to a large extent upon the type of work in which
the helper is involved. Pastors, social workers, doctors or health
visitors sometimes see people in their own offices, sometimes in an
office which is shared with others (even if they are absent at the
time), and sometimes in their 'client's' own home. Seeing a person

at home requires particular consideration, although it sometimes has the advantage of giving the helper a better understanding of their physical situation and some of the pressures with which they live each day. However, it is also much more difficult to control interruptions, and it may be more difficult to control the timing of an interview without making the time boundaries crystal clear from the start, and keeping to them. Seeing people in the helper's office can also involve interruptions, although generally it is easier to control these. Telephones may be intercepted before they ring in the office, or an answering machine can take the call that would otherwise disrupt the meeting. When someone is visited in their home they may not be so adept at coping with interruptions – so meeting people on neutral ground can help them to take a step back from their domestic or working situation and see things more clearly.

It is usually helpful to set a clear time limit on an interview, especially if the person seeking help is anxious about taking up time, or does not appear to recognize that the helper has other duties. This may be negotiated before meeting by asking a person how much time they think they would like; or it can be stated at the start of the meeting. Such boundaries help both parties to engage fully in the time available, knowing the inevitability of having to finish at a particular time. A time limit may encourage the speaker to come out with what is most important to them, rather than put it off with small talk. There is no reason why any of these arrangements cannot be made in a relaxed and natural way.

If the interview takes place in the helper's office, it is possible to arrange the seating so that both parties are on equal terms. If upright chairs have to be used, and there is a desk in the room, it is better to avoid interposing this as a barrier between the listener and the speaker. It may be possible to arrange the chairs so that the visitor is not distracted by signs of 'business'. If the listener sits with a wall chart behind her or his back, it is easy to imagine how the speaker's attention might wander off, especially if the listener is trying to express something that is difficult to hear. Research, as well as experience, suggests that babies feed better when the mother does not, on the one hand, look at her infant the whole time or, on the other hand, spend all the time looking distractedly around the room. Eye contact is important, but should never be overdone. While it is important to observe the speaker, it is not helpful to stare; eye contact which shifts smoothly to and away from the speaker is much less inquisitorial and confrontational. Placing chairs in a good position allows both the speaker and listener to look at each other when they both wish, but also allows one to look at the other while the latter looks away, or both to look away from each other, so that continual and more relaxed eye movement is taking place.

Exercise 9

It is possible to experiment with seating positions in this exercise, which also provides an opportunity to practise tolerating short silences. If several pairs are involved a timekeeper is useful. Sufficient space between pairs is also necessary for chairs to be moved easily.

The exercise starts by forming pairs, whose chairs are positioned (i) in the diagram.

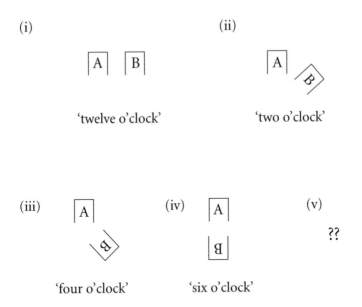

(i)

A   B

'twelve o'clock'

(ii)

A B

'two o'clock'

(iii) A

B

'four o'clock'

(iv) A

B

'six o'clock'

(v)

??

The pairs sit quietly for half a minute in the twelve o'clock position and when the time is called discuss together how they felt, and feel, for a further half minute (not yet moving the chairs). When time is called (at the end of the further half minute), B moves to sit in the two o'clock position (ii). Again spend half a minute in silence, and when time is called share how that position felt and feels. Again, when time is called, B moves to the four o'clock position (iii), again for half a minute of silence, and half a minute spent talking about it; then B moves to the six o'clock position (iv), for a further half-minute of silence, and half-minute sharing what that was like. Finally, for the fifth position (v), both partners in the pair should move their chairs until both feel they have found the best position – one which permits them to feel relatively more comfortable than any other, both for the silent times and for speaking together. Where there are several pairs taking part in this exercise, the pairs should look around and see which arrangement appears to be the most popular.

Long use of this exercise suggests that most pairs prefer the four o'clock position, which generally avoids eyeball-to-eyeball observation. The six o'clock position is rarely chosen, except by offsetting the chairs so that each person can look past the other:

$$\boxed{A}$$

$$\boxed{\text{ᗺ}}$$

There are some exceptions to the preferred position, but it is worth remembering that even if some helpers feel more comfortable in a different position, the balance of opinion is in favour of the four o'clock arrangement, which suggests that this might suit the majority of those who come to seek help. However in working with certain groups of people – such as those with impaired hearing or sight, or the elderly – a closer arrangement of the chairs (such as the two o'clock position) may be more practical.

Summary

'To hear, one must be silent', says a wise man to his apprentice in Le Guin's fantasy novel *A Wizard of Earthsea*.[4] This silence extends to calmness within the listener, as far as possible in a setting that is quiet. Yet such silence is far from passive: active listening, alert watching, and thoughtful monitoring of yourself constitute the skills of listening, enabling those who are asked to help to hear better what people really want to say. Only then does the helper presume to speak, drawing on guidelines that are examined in detail in the next chapter.

THREE

Guidelines for Responding

---

8. Use words carefully; be as accurate as possible in describing feelings and ideas that you perceive (not just 'depressed' or 'angry')

When the listener has heard what the person seeking help has said, has listened for underlying feelings and thoughts which have not yet been openly voiced, he or she will want to respond. There are many ways of doing this productively, but common to them all is the attempt to identify as accurately as possible the feelings and ideas that are in one way or another being expressed.

There is a tendency in all walks of life towards jargon, and the world of counselling is no exception. Apart from technical terms, it is easy to slip into a narrow set of descriptions of what people are feeling: common adjectives like 'depressed' or 'angry' (or in America the word 'hostile') can be stretched to cover many variations on a mood. Despite the difficulty of putting feelings into words, there is an immensely rich vocabulary with which to describe the shades of feelings that people are experiencing. 'Depressed' might well be avoided in favour of the gradation of feelings from being low through to deeper despair; and 'angry' is too often used as a blanket term, when the feelings range from mild irritation through to blind rage and murderous hatred.

There are good reasons for attempting to find the right words to describe what someone is saying or feeling. If, in responding to someone describing their situation, the carer uses terms that are too heavy, the speaker is quite likely to reject such a description. 'You seem *furious* about missing the train' will surely meet with puzzlement or appropriate denial if the person made it clear they were only annoyed about it; but it is possible that in denying the fury they will also deny being annoyed. On the other hand, if the response does not give sufficient recognition to the strength of feeling, then this strength is less easily acknowledged. 'You seem *upset* about the divorce' might receive assent, but at the same time an opportunity could have been lost to allow the full feelings to be expressed – for instance, this person might be *very distressed*. If the listener recognizes the feeling accurately, then the speaker can respond more readily with their true feelings. To be accurate is all the more necessary when you are suggesting a feeling or thought that has not been openly acknowledged. There is then more chance that it can be owned, and perhaps further explored.

Furthermore, there are subtleties in shades of feeling which mean that what appears as one obvious emotion might be masking another. Is a person trembling with fear or with rage? Is a person upset because they think they are going to be told off, or because they are experiencing grief? The following exercise attempts to examine the variety of terms which can be used to express variations on common moods. It also aims to help you identify the shades of feeling which might be present in a particular set of actions.

Exercise 10

Adjectives are used to qualify nouns and adverbs to qualify verbs – in other words, to provide a much more accurate description. This variation on a party game uses these forms to demonstrate the wide vocabulary which can be used to describe feeling.

Form into a group or groups of six or seven and choose a group leader, who is going to make a record of the progress of this exercise. The leader asks one or two of the group members to leave the room (two is preferable, to provide help for each other), and in their absence the rest of the group decide upon an adjective or adverb which they will try to portray when the members are called back. The returning members then ask one or more of the group members to perform an action to demonstrate the word chosen. For example, if 'angry' has been chosen, those trying to guess it might ask two people to talk together in the manner of this word: they will then guess what the word is, and the leader makes a note of the guess. Another action is then requested from another member or members; and so it goes on until the word is guessed, or until ten guesses have been made. The leader then reads out the list of words which were thrown up in relation to the original word chosen by the group. These may represent shades of a particular mood, or may show that similar actions can elicit quite different descriptions. A further one or two members leave the group, who decide a new word in their absence, they return, and so on. This game calls for considerable imagination in requesting the actions to be performed, but can be fun especially if people in the group can let themselves be fairly uninhibited.

Groups might like to draw on the following adjectives. It is possible to play this with the leader being in charge of the list, informing the group, each time two members leave the room, of the next word to enact.

hesitant	resentful	weary
contented	thoughtful	charming

Where several groups can be formed and a common list such as this has been devised by the trainer, comparisons can be made of each group's lists. The learning outcome of this exercise is not so much the ability to guess the correct word as the opportunity to see what variations there are around one adjective. It has a different aim from the non-verbal communication of Exercises 5 and 6. There the goal was identify basic moods. In this exercise the emphasis is on learning how fine are the lines that make for good reflective responses.

9. Use your empathic understanding, again making this accurate, although also tentative (you may be wrong)

The first steps towards empathy have been outlined in Chapter 2 (described in Guideline 5, and practised in Exercise 8). Empathic responses are a very important part of counselling, and can be valuable in any interview where the listener is encouraging the expression of feelings. Empathy is always a *tentative* attempt to put into words what the other person is feeling; it can be reflected back to the person telling their story in a number of ways:

1. Sometimes it is so obvious what a person is feeling that an empathic response can be definite: 'You are obviously very upset by this . . .'

2. Being definite is risky if there is any doubt, or if helpers imagine they 'know' what the other is feeling. It is often better to clarify a hunch as to what a person might be feeling through a question, such as, 'Do you think you might be feeling somewhat anxious as

well as excited by . . . ?' – or by waiting for more confirmation as the story develops before making an empathic response.

3. It can also be helpful to phrase an empathic response so that the other person can choose to disagree if it is wrong. 'You seem to be calm about this, but I wonder whether you might also be feeling quite bitter?' Words such as 'perhaps', 'I'm not sure but I guess', or 'maybe' serve the same purpose. Many people in caring or helping positions are potent figures to those who ask for their help. Some people agree with whatever is said to them, even if later they have second thoughts. A good listener does not try to force an opinion on the other, but tries to draw the other out; and the listener who is prepared to be wrong may find that the speaker is prepared to accept part of what is reflected back, but can then qualify it, making it more accurate for themselves. For example:

LISTENER I am wondering whether you are upset at not getting that job.
SPEAKER I'm not sure – I don't think I'd say I'm upset.
Actually I am pretty annoyed at the way I performed at the interview . . .

Exercise 11

Empathy involves an attempt to enter into another person's experience, and to feel and think as that person might: it means trying to feel what it might be like to be in their shoes. This may be easier if the listener has experienced a similar situation to that which the speaker describes, although I have already cautioned against identifying too closely in the belief that one person's experience is the same as another's. Whether or not the helper has had a similar experience, considerable imagination is needed to identify *accurately* what the other person might be feeling.

In this exercise start by forming pairs, and spending some five minutes finding an experience which one partner has had but which is foreign to the other. Each can then take a turn in trying to describe what the other's experience may have been like. For example, partner A may have been in hospital, and partner B may only know hospitals from visiting others; while partner B may be of a different ethnic group from partner A. First identify these 'unique' experiences. B then thinks aloud, trying to identify what it might be like to be in hospital. A should not interrupt these reflections, but should allow B to speak for a few minutes. Only when B has finished does A feed back what felt accurate in B's description, and what was not; and what was not their own experience but may be others' experience in the same situation. Reverse roles, so that A reflects aloud to B on what it might be like to be a member of a different ethnic group.

When both partners have had their turn, there is room for useful discussion about how far it is possible to be empathic towards others who have apparently different experiences: for example, can men identify empathically with women and vice versa, black people with Asian people, etc.?

10. Keep questions to a minimum ...

Interviews often consist of a series of questions and answers – and normally it is the interviewer who asks the questions. This may be because many interviews are concerned with gleaning as much relevant information as possible in the time available, whether it be an interview for a job, an interview to make arrangements for a wedding, or an interview with a doctor or a lawyer. Given time constraints, this is understandable – although it is not the only way of gathering information.

Since a helper's concern is to listen and reflect accurately as a way of promoting communication, even when a clear request for advice has been made by the client, it is worth observing that questions do not have to predominate. Old habits die hard, and the greatest temptation for any helper is to listen for a while, but then to launch into a long series of questions. Sometimes helpers do not even listen fully to the answers, but interrupt an answer with yet another question they feel they ought to ask, rather than taking up what is being talked about.

This becomes very obvious in the next chapter, when exercises lead on to practising all the guidelines in the context of one interview. A chart counts the types of intervention made by the helper, and it tends to have one line which is ticked more frequently than the others – the line recording each time the helper asks a question.

There are much better ways of responding than asking questions, as shown in all the other guidelines in this chapter. However, there

clearly are times when a question might be helpful, and when it is
necessary the following guidelines apply.

. . . *unless you need precise information (in which case ask precise questions)*

When the helper wishes to find out more about an event, a person,
or any of the other details which come out of an interview or conversation, it is right to ask a question, as long as it is precise and one
question is asked (and answered) at a time. This type of question is
called 'closed', and may not be mentioned often in counselling
literature, where the assumption is frequently that the only valid
questions are open-ended. Yet helpers may need definite information
– and they can ask for it, as long as this type of question does not
predominate. Examples of closed questions, where the answer is
fairly straightforward and are often factual, are: 'How long has this
been going on?'; 'What was the name of the doctor whom you saw?';
'What do you do for a living?'; 'What time shall we arrange to meet
again?'; 'How many children do you have?'

   Necessary though such questions are, it is important not to become
hooked on them. Most helpers are not required to take a detailed
case history – and even if they are, they can often find out just as
much by permitting the person to speak freely, with occasional
questions for clarification, and occasional nudges in the direction
where it feels that certain information might help.

. . . *unless you want to open up an area (in which case use open-ended questions)*

Good precise questions should reveal precise information. Questions
can also be used in a more open way, whereby the person telling
their story is invited to take up any aspect of the question that they
wish. Many closed questions begin with 'how (long, much), who,
what, when, where, etc. – and such questions immediately impose
some limitation on the answer. For instance, if someone says, 'I get
depressed', one response is to ask questions which are somewhat
closed: 'When do you get depressed?'; 'What makes you depressed?;
'Who makes you depressed?'; or 'How long have you been
depressed?' It is possible, and perhaps preferable, to ask a more open
question which allows the speaker to pursue their own answer: such

as, 'Would you like to tell me more about being depressed?' This invites the person to answer, rather than requires them to do so. And it does not suggest a particular piece of information which the helper wants to hear. The person can take the word 'depressed' where they want: what it feels like, what triggers it, how long it has been this way, etc. Therefore if a helper wants to open up a particular area and does not require precise information, they should make their questions (if they use questions at all) as open as possible, able to lead anywhere.

. . . unless you wish to prompt (when rhetorical questions help)

Perhaps the most effective open-ended questions are those which are very short and are apparently rhetorical (i.e. they presume the answer 'yes' or 'no'). They often enable the helper to pursue a line without appearing to press it. A very useful linguistic device is to repeat the last word, or last few words, in the form of a question:

SPEAKER   I get depressed.
LISTENER Depressed?

Naturally, the listener's selection of an interrogative phrase can limit the answer somewhat. 'I get very depressed sometimes at work', Barbara says. Her GP will get back a slightly different answer depending upon the phrase they pick up, which could be 'Very?', 'Very depressed?', 'Sometimes?' or 'At work?' The most open question in response to what Barbara has said, which does not suggest that she answer in any particular way, is one which picks up the whole phrase: 'You get very depressed sometimes at work?' – said in an even tone throughout, without any particular emphasis.

. . . and avoid at all costs questions beginning 'Why . . . ?'

'Why?' And if the reader asks this question, I feel I have to supply a reasonable explanation. This is indeed the difficulty with the question 'why?'. This particular form of interrogative asks for an explanation, which in this case I am giving, but which people in distress often do not. 'I am depressed', says Barbara to her doctor. 'Why are you depressed?' replies the doctor. 'If I knew that I wouldn't be here', Barbara replies with justified feeling. Asking the question 'why?' is risky, because while it is possible that the person knows the answer, it is equally possible that he or she does not, and may even feel foolish that they cannot answer what on the surface appears such a straightforward question.

There is a further reason for avoiding this form of question. It is often associated with a somewhat critical, even aggressive stance on the part of the questioner, reminiscent no doubt of childhood and of being asked 'why?' when something went wrong.

CHILD   I've dropped the plate and broken it.
PARENT   Why did you drop it?
CHILD   I don't know, but it was an accident.
PARENT   But why?

And so it goes on . . .

Obviously much depends on the way any question is asked, and sometimes a 'why' question is appropriate. Yet it is better to avoid what can be a particularly tricky question, as well as one that tends to look for an intellectual explanation, rather than really exploring further thoughts and feelings.

Exercise 12

This exercise needs to be set up by a trainer or group leader, without the participants seeing all three roles set out below. The group is split up into threes, and each member of each trio is given a separate set of instructions. Only B and C know what is going on beneath the obvious instructions. It is important to have a time limit of five minutes, followed by discussion, particularly with C sharing observations on the way in which A and B coped with the increasing silences (if indeed B could allow the silences to become longer: in fact B is under just as much pressure to speak, despite knowing the secret instructions).

Partner A: Your partner B is pretending to be a person he or she knows, but whom you do not know. You have no more than five minutes to ask questions of a straightforward, factual nature, which you address to your partner B in an endeavour to find out as much as you can about the person. If your partner does not answer your question, to which he or she may say 'Pass', then ask another. Do not ask questions which could lead to any embarrassment.

Partner B: Imagine you are someone you know, but whom your partner A does not know. Your partner is going to ask you a series of questions of a straightforward nature. Answer the questions, although if there is a question you do not want to or cannot answer, say 'Pass'. But please follow the next instruction very carefully: after every question from your partner allow one second more before you answer it or before you say 'Pass' – i.e. one second before you answer the first question, two seconds before you answer the second, and so on. Count the seconds in your head: saying the words 'One hundred, two hundred, etc.' is a good way of doing this. If your partner asks you a further question before you have finished counting, start the counting all over again and add one more second.

Partner C: You are the observer. This exercise is only partially about questions; it is also another way of seeing whether the questioner can allow enough silence for the person answering to reply. The person answering has been told to allow one second more for each question before replying – i.e. one second after the first question, two after the second, etc. Record the number of questions asked. But also watch both people to see how relaxed they stay, or how agitated they become as the silences get longer over the five-minute period. When time is called, explain to the questioner what has been going on, and share your observations on the ability of each of them to tolerate (or not) the silences, and help them to share how they felt as time went on.

This exercise also highlights just how futile some questions are, and how monotonous a series of questions and answers can become.

Exercise 13

This exercise really *is* about questions, looking at the difference between open and closed questions. In pairs, or small groups, take one or more of the following statements and draw up a series of questions, ranging from the most closed and most precise question (remembering that this particular information may be important) to the most open type of question. No more than five questions will illustrate the difference.

Example:	'I'm sorry I'm late.'
closed	(a) Did you miss the bus again?
↓	(b) Have there been problems?
	(c) What happened?
open	(d) You're sorry you're late?

Draw up a similar set in response to the following statements:

1. 'I get very angry sometimes at home.'
2. 'I don't like the services at St Cuthbert's.'
3. 'I'm afraid I'm not going to pass the exam.'
4. 'I'm feeling very ill.'
5. 'I want a transfer out of this department.'

Exercise 14

There are other ways of eliciting information from people without appearing to become an inquisitor. This exercise practises ways of doing this.

Questions are such a common feature of interviewing and of ordinary conversations that it is not surprising that helpers are conditioned to over-use them in responding to people. This compulsion to ask questions also applies to answering them – so people who ask for help may feel that a question demands an answer, although a question (however well-intentioned) may also put the one who is questioned on the defensive. In this exercise alternative and less threatening ways of gaining information are used.

Some alternatives to asking questions include:

1. Observing non-verbal clues. Instead of asking 'What's upsetting you?', the helper can say, 'You appear to be upset'. This invites the person to say what he or she is feeling upset about – but does not demand it. 'Appear' refers to actual appearance but also conveys the tentativeness of the response.

2. Closely related are 'seem to be' statements, which may observe non-verbal clues, but essentially draw upon empathic understanding of what lies behind the person's tone of voice or choice of

words. Instead of asking: 'What's troubling you?', the helper chooses an empathic comment, again inviting the person to take it further if they wish: 'You seem to be troubled'.

3. The use of 'I' statements. Here the helper uses a modified form of self-disclosure in order to draw the client into explaining more about a situation. Instead of asking 'Why didn't you get angry with him?', a helper can describe their own reaction: 'I found myself getting angry as you told me that'. Or instead of asking, 'What happened before you met him?', the helper can express a more personal interest: 'I think I would find it helpful to know more about what life was like for you before you met, if you feel you could tell me'.

4. An invitation to answer a question is always far less threatening than even the most necessary question: 'Only answer this if you feel you want to, but what is the relationship with your mother like?' Although the shorthand 'Tell me about' statement sounds as bald as a question, it is softer to combine it with an invitation: so instead of asking 'What about your father?', a carer might say, 'Perhaps you could tell me about your father'; or (still a question, but much softer): 'Would you like to tell me about your father?'

5. Use minimal responses (see Guideline 11), inviting the person to take further what he or she has just been saying, perhaps (though perhaps not, it is up to the person) in the direction the helper's question might have moved it. Thus, instead of asking a supplementary question, the counsellor simply says 'Yes . . .' or 'No . . .'; or (gently) 'Go on . . .'

6. An additional way of minimally inviting the client to say more rather than ask a question is to use a gesture or facial expression, a slight movement of the hand, or raising the eyebrows a little in a questioning expression.

The group is once more divided into pairs. Each pair devises a brief conversation in which the questions below are replaced by other forms of gaining the same information. Each pair is to write a brief script, where one partner is the questioner and the other is invited to say more. Try using a different alternative to a question for each of the five parts of the conversation. The pairs rehearse the short script briefly, and then form into small groups consisting of three or four pairs, where they demonstrate to each other their alternatives to questions, and their version of how this conversation might go.

1. How did you get that plaster on your arm?
2. What speed were you doing at the time?
3. What happened after you hit the car?
4. Did you feel angry about that?
5. Did you think it was his fault?

One possible conversation, avoiding the explicit questions, might run as follows:

1. *How did you get that plaster on your arm?*
   A [*Noticing plaster on B's arm*] You look as if you've been in the wars.
   B Well, it feels like it. Actually I was involved in an accident. I collided with another car.

2. *What speed were you doing at the time?*
   A One of you must have been going quite fast to get an injury like that.
   B Well, it was only 40 miles an hour, but he swerved out in front of me.

3. *What happened after you hit the car?*
   A Uh-huh . . .
   B He got out and walked over to me as right as rain and asked me whether I was hurt. It was my new car; I could have wept.

4. *Did you feel angry about that?*
   A I'd have felt furious about that.
   B Yes, I suppose I was too – although at the time my main worry was that I, of course, was the person coming up behind him.

5. *Did you think it was his fault?*
   A You sound concerned in case *you're* blamed for the accident.
   B Yes, it was quite clearly his fault.

Exercise 15

This exercise suggests that there are ways other than the obvious ones of understanding the questions which people sometimes ask the helper; it gives practice in devising more useful responses than just addressing the questions at face value.

When someone seeking help asks a question it can often have more than one level. While a straight answer may be all that is required, the question might mean something else. In everyday conversations people have learned to ask questions rather than communicate more directly what they would like to say. For example, a parent may ask a teenager 'Where are you going?', when the parent really wants to say, 'I wish you'd stay and help me with the washing-up'. Or someone may say to a friend, 'What are you doing tonight?', when they would prefer to say, 'I rather like you and would like go out with you'. Or in a committee meeting one member may ask, 'What's the time?', when they really mean, 'What a boring meeting! How much longer is it going on for?'

Sometimes it is important not to frustrate unnecessarily and so a client's question needs to be answered. But at other times it is not appropriate to answer it, or it is more important, at least for the time being, to get at what the question might signify. There are, therefore, three ways of responding to a question addressed to the helper:

1. to answer it, and then to look at what else the question might mean;
2. to look at what it might mean and answer it after that;
3. to look at what the question might mean, and in doing so render the original answer to it unnecessary (perhaps the most common of the three).

There is a great difference between answering a question and actually responding to it. The best response is the one which in some way satisfies what the person is really wanting. In this context their question might be met with a question – although, as the previous exercise illustrates, it is less combative when the helper's alternative answer is also an alternative to a question! In order to identify what a person might be saying when asking a question, it is worth considering some possible responses to the possible meanings behind a person asking the carer, 'Do you want to see me again?'

(a) The helper may respond with a statement about intent: 'You seem to think you've got to come back to see me'.

(b) The helper may respond with a statement about the emotional state of the person: 'You sound rather anxious'.

(c) The helper may respond with a generic, inclusive comment: 'People are often not sure whether they can come back another time'.

(d) The helper may comment on the process: 'It feels like it's difficult to leave it there'.

(e) The helper may not be clear about the meaning and ask for clarification, putting the question back: 'I wonder what you yourself want?'

In this exercise form pairs or threes to consider what the person who has come for help might be asking in each of the following questions; and devise one alternative response that might be used in reply to each question. Where possible, use a variety of responses, which between them demonstrate each of the possible meanings behind a question, as listed above.

1. Do you think I'm crazy?
2. Would you suggest I change my job?
3. What sort of training have you had for your job?
4. Do you ever shout at your children?
5. How much longer have I got this morning?

Feedback will illustrate the variety of ways of interpreting some of the questions people ask their helpers. It is also possible to work on some of the difficult questions which those in the group are asked when they are in their caring role.

The following list includes examples of the five types of response outlined above, as they might be used in interpreting these different questions:

1. Do you think I'm crazy?
    (b) You appear very frightened by how you are feeling.
    (d) You always seem to worry about that when you talk about your family.
    (e) What do you mean by 'crazy'?

2. *Would you suggest I change my job?*
    (a) You seem to want me to give you definite advice.
    (b) You look anxious about that possibility.
    (c) People sometimes ask that rather than look at what they might change about their present work.

3. *What sort of training have you had for your job?*
    (a) Perhaps you are wondering whether I will be able to help.
    (c) People sometimes ask me that when they've got something really worrying on their minds.
    (e) I wonder what you're really saying when you ask that?

4. *Do you ever shout at your children?*
    (b) You're looking cross with me at the moment.
    (c) Nearly everybody does. Perhaps it worries you?
    (d) Do I appear to be angry with you?

5. *How much longer have I got this morning?*
    (a) You seem to think you have to stay.
    (b) You look worried at having to leave.
    (d) I notice you tend to ask that when there's something you're not sure about mentioning.

11. Use minimal prompts: 'Mm', 'Yes', or repeat the last few words

As might be expected of this guideline, there is really very little to be said. Minimal prompts not only include saying 'Mm' and 'Yes' while the speaker is talking, but also when the speaker finishes or pauses. Such prompts can help the speaker to go on with what they were saying. Another very effective way of gently guiding a person into saying more is to take up the last few words, not so much in question form (which we considered above) but as a simple statement. Here again much depends on which phrase the listener chooses to highlight, since the emphasis the listener gives to one word in a sentence rather than another will inevitably suggest a particular direction. It is possible, through using a minimal prompt of the last few words, to help a person to go on speaking, constantly expanding. For example:

SPEAKER   I'm afraid I was unable to do what you asked.
HELPER   Unable to do it.

SPEAKER Yes, I went round to the house but there was some local difficulty.

HELPER *Local* difficulty.

SPEAKER Yes, it appears there was a fire in the warehouse nearby and all the residents had been evacuated. I found out that they'd been moved to a local hall, but he wasn't there.

HELPER He *wasn't* there.

SPEAKER No, it's possible that he was on holiday, but no one was really sure of his plans. I think this latest business must have thrown him.

. . . and so on.

This is such a simple way of encouraging people to say more that it scarcely needs practice, although many helpers respond by saying much more than they need. It needs to be used naturally, and not parrot fashion. Used sensitively in this way minimal prompts can move a conversation remarkably far, with the helper uttering very little – although it remains important to indicate in expression and tone of voice that they are interested and listening.

12. Paraphrase or reflect accurately as: a way of prompting: an indication that you have been listening: a way of checking out that you have heard correctly

Whether someone speaks briefly and then stops, or whether they talk for several minutes before pausing, the use of paraphrase or a combination of précis and paraphrase makes an effective response which serves three purposes:

1. Like the 'last few words' in the last section, and the rhetorical question that uses just a short phrase, it is a way of prompting the person to say more.
2. A paraphrase, by definition, needs to be an accurate re-statement of what the speaker has said, and so it acts as a signal that the helper has been listening.
3. It provides an opportunity for checking out that the person speaking has been heard correctly.

In addition, this type of summary can act as a sounding board so that the speaker not only hears himself or herself saying the words, but then hears them 'played back'. It is surprising how often such a reflection makes a person stop and think, and then perhaps add a new dimension to their thinking. It may even prove a more effective response than trying to persuade the speaker to hold a different point of view.

For example, the speaker may say in an unguarded moment, 'I can't stand black people taking over this country'. Here is a remark which could easily cause the helper's hackles to rise, and which suggests that the helper should issue some corrective statement to try and put the other point of view. If, however, the person listening can respond in the calm and accepting way which is a constant feature of good facilitating, they may simply reply, 'You feel black people are taking us over?' By its very starkness this brief response might enable the speaker to see how prejudiced and exaggerated their original statement was. So the speaker replies, 'Well, I don't want you to think I'm a racist, but . . .' Yet the damage has already been done, and the speaker has already (we hope) begun to recognize and confront a part of himself. A further example: a university student says to his tutor, 'I'm awfully sorry, but I can't hand that project in today, because . . .', and he reels off a list of fairly trivial reasons. Instead of the tutor replying, as well she might, 'All that sounds pretty thin to me', she simply restates the reasons that the student has given. 'Well,' says the student, 'they sound just like excuses, but . . .' The tutor hears him out, and then perhaps asks, 'Well, what's the real reason, do you think?'

Attacking a person's statements often leads to argument, defensiveness and denial. Going along with what the person has said, by simply reflecting it back, is not always collusive, but often faces them with what they have said and suggests to them that they may need to look at what they have expressed.

Exercise 16

Each section of this exercise contains an initial statement, and a list of eight responses which the helper might make. Some of those responses are potentially useful, but a few are not at all right. The object of this exercise is to select the response which is the *most accurate paraphrase* of the initial statement. It is not to select the most effective response (which may be an empathic response, or a good question), but to decide which is the most accurate paraphrase.

With the exception of the first example (where the best paraphrase is fairly obvious), the remaining examples are not clear cut. Where participants in this exercise are working in small groups, they need to put forward arguments *for* the statement they have chosen as the best paraphrase, and *against* those opinions which differ from them; and finally they should collaborate in putting together a composite statement which is a truly accurate paraphrase of the original statement.

1. I wish I didn't find it so difficult to concentrate properly on my job, but my father is ill in hospital, and I can't help worrying about him all the time.

   (a) You don't want to work when you're feeling so worried about him.
   (b) We can't afford to have people here who don't do their job.
   (c) You'd like some compassionate leave while your father's ill.
   (d) You're concerned that your father is so very ill.
   (e) Try working a little harder, so you can forget about him while you're here. Worry doesn't do him any good.
   (f) You feel pulled between your loyalty to the firm and your loyalty to him.
   (g) I know what it's like – I felt the same when my child was in hospital.
   (h) Worrying about your father makes it difficult to give your mind to the work.

2. I don't want to appear to be against the young people, but I do think we should do something about those teenagers who sit in the back row of the church and chew gum, talk and hold hands.

   (a) You're disturbed by the young people who come to church.
   (b) You were young once, or perhaps you don't remember?
   (c) I agree, but I don't want to reject them just because they don't conform.
   (d) You're shocked by the behaviour of some of the young people today.
   (e) What do you suggest we do about it?
   (f) You don't like people who don't take worship seriously.
   (g) You want me to ask them to behave properly in church.
   (h) Perhaps that makes it difficult for you to worship with us.

3. My best friend tells me that my boyfriend back home is going out with another girl, but my boyfriend denies it. He says he's longing for me to be home.

   (a) You must be very worried.
   (b) Just like a man to treat women like that.
   (c) You don't believe your boyfriend.
   (d) You feel angry at your best friend telling tales about your boyfriend.
   (e) I should get another boyfriend, and make the one at home feel jealous too.
   (f) You don't know whom to trust, your best friend or your boyfriend.
   (g) It's difficult being so far away that you don't know what's going on.
   (h) You can't wait to get home to him too.

4. I find all this race relations business difficult. I went on an equal opportunities course the other day, but I just don't believe black and white people are really able to understand one another.

   (a) You are worried that people from different racial backgrounds will not be able to work together.
   (b) You don't think that black people can get on with white people.
   (c) I think that's a very pessimistic picture.
   (d) You're not in favour of equal opportunities policies.
   (e) After attending the training you wondered whether harmony was possible.
   (f) Perhaps you are unsure about whether you want to work with people who are different.
   (g) I think we should leave it there, and not talk about it in case we're prejudiced.
   (h) You feel the training showed how difficult it is for some people to work together.

5. I really loathe this town – it was good to find a job, but it meant we had to move here. The place is so drab and lifeless – it makes it so difficult to feel friendly to people.

   (a) You hate everything about living here.
   (b) You were forced to move here and resent that a lot.

   (c) You have to live here, but you can't stand the place or the
      people.
   (d) Why don't you try talking to people? They may not be as
      drab as the town.
   (e) You're feeling down, and that makes it difficult to relate to
      people.
   (f) It's a dreadful situation to be in, isn't it?
   (g) You're trying to weigh up the advantages and disadvantages
      of living here.
   (h) It sounds like there's been a lot of upheaval for you lately.

13. Avoid making judgements or loaded remarks

It is important to be able to make the right response to others – but
it is probably even more important to *avoid* making remarks which
erect an immediate barrier to further communication, or which at
best do not help promote communication. Here therefore we consider a number of particular guidelines, some of which are very
obvious and others of which require explanation. These guidelines
are followed by an exercise which considers both inappropriate and
appropriate responses.

Avoid exclamations of surprise, intolerance or disgust

There is a story of a young Catholic priest who was hearing his first
confessions, and had a senior priest listening in on him in order to
give him some guidance afterwards (which in itself suggests it is far
from true!). After hearing an hour's confessions, the young priest
returned to the sacristy with his mentor and asked him, 'How did I
do, Father?' 'Fairly well', replied the older man, 'but next time a little
more of the "tut, tuts" and a little less of the "phews"'!
   Neither surprise nor horror, disgust nor salacious interest, have
any place in the responses of the helper. This does not mean that in
listening to some people such *feelings* do not arise. These reactions
are human, and probably indicate the gravity of a situation. Nor
does failure to show such feelings mean that all behaviours which
give rise to them are being condoned. Rather the helper needs to try
to see the situation from another point of view: without endorsing
actual or verbal violence, racism, sexism, etc., the listener, by stretch-
ing the power of their empathy, might be able to see such strong and

undesirable feelings as themselves being a response to deprivation, frustration, etc.

Needless to say, it is not simply verbal responses of surprise or shock which need to be avoided. It is also the *non-verbal* reactions – such as facial expression, or rapid change of posture, abruptness of tone of voice and so on, all of which might indicate to the speaker that the helper has turned against them on account of what they have said. It is easier to suggest the importance of avoiding such responses than it is to prescribe what should be said, although the exercise that follows provides an opportunity to try out more appropriate responses.

Avoid expressions of over-concern

The stress here is to avoid *over*-concern. Concern which is too effusive, even sympathy ('Oh, I *am* sorry') may sound patronizing; it may also sound (and indeed often is) a well-meaning substitute for the inability to help. We cannot change a situation, and feel we must say something passionately to compensate for our helplessness. The speaker may validly reply (sometimes silently), 'It's not sympathy I want. I want something done about it.' In such circumstances an empathic response (even if not changing the situation) stands more chance of reaching into the speaker's present experience – for example, 'You must be feeling very disappointed'. It may even be more honest to say, 'I am not sure how I can best help in this situation'.

Nevertheless there are times when it is right to express reassurance or sympathy because it really seems necessary. When a helper genuinely feels sympathy for the person speaking (rather than anxiety that they do not know how to help), a quiet 'I'm sorry', or putting together both the bleakness of the present situation with any positive features there may be, is appropriate: 'It must be terrible hearing the news of your son's accident; it's small consolation, although it is something, to know that he is going to be all right.'

Avoid moralistic judgements, criticism or impatience

Good listening can help others to make their own judgements about what to do in a more rational frame of mind. Talking takes the heat out of the situation, and as emotions are expressed, it becomes easier

to think. Many of those who seek help when things have gone
wrong do not need someone else to point out to them where they
have made mistakes. It is more often those who do not seek help
who need attention drawn to their behaviour. While the listener
may be aware of making moral judgements, and perhaps wanting
to criticize certain actions, whether they have been done or are
proposed, a better way is to put the assessment of the situation back
to the speaker: 'How did (or do) you feel about that? Do you think
that is the right thing to do? What's to be said for and against that
choice of action?' The listener tries to elevate moral thinking and
decision making to an adult level, and keep away from the parental
role which the 'wayward child' aspect in the story might engender in
the carer as authority figure.

Avoid being defensive and getting caught up in arguments

When people feel criticized by others, one method of self-defence is
attack. Another is to get caught up in an argument in which particular words and phrases become the central issue, and the situation
which gave rise to the original criticism is forgotten. When the
helper responds, and receives back a hostile or quibbling answer, it
does not matter how correct the response was. No amount of argument will make the point. Even if the helper wins the ensuing
argument on points, the person who felt criticized will in all likeli-
hood go away feeling resentful or misunderstood. Fraught situations
need to be kept cool, and may even need to be put on ice for a while
to allow strong emotions to subside, before they can be looked at
more dispassionately.

Avoid colluding, but remain open-minded, even towards irrational attitudes or different values and opinions

In listening to others the helper is not required to agree with everything they say. Indeed it is important not to collude with people
who come out with what appear to the listener to be crazy ideas,
false conclusions or conflicting beliefs. But to challenge some
opinions might simply lead to a destructive argument (as already
mentioned). Often it is simply enough to listen, even to nod to show
attention, without signifying agreement. Those who learn to listen
at a deeper level can sometimes find good reasons why people hold

what at first appear to be strange views. The helper can sometimes introduce contrasting views, which might make for more balanced understanding, by first demonstrating that they have heard the speaker's opinion and then putting the other side – for example, 'I realize that you feel very strongly about this. It's difficult when there are different ways of looking at the problem, like . . .'

The helper may be asked whether they agree with a statement which they find distasteful or believe to be wrong. With experience it becomes easy to deflect such questions; for example, in response to the question 'I think that all murderers should be hanged, don't you agree?', various replies could include 'That's what you think?'; 'You feel the need for revenge?'; or 'Does it matter to you whether I agree or not?'

Avoid false promises, or flattery or undue praise

False promises, flattery and undue praise all have a parental quality about them: the helper becomes like a parent who promises a child a treat in order to quieten his tantrum or allay her anxiety. The condescending expression of praise is felt to be false, because the child does not feel pleased or proud or comforted. 'I think it is very good to have got as far as a short list' is no consolation to the person who is still without a job. Even where the situation gives the helper some pleasure (perhaps the person they have been helping returns to share good news), too ready an offer of congratulations may make the helper appear to be a parental figure who is there to be pleased. An empathic response, or an open question, is a far better response: 'You must be pleased', or 'How do you feel about that?' The latter is sometimes a safer response to make, because what seems an achievement to the listener might be felt (albeit unrealistically) as a failure to the speaker: for example, 'You must have been very pleased with that result'. 'No, I expected to get a distinction.'

Avoid ridicule, condescension or belittling the person

This guideline is a variation on those described above: do not be over-concerned and do not give undue praise. Ridicule is a more obvious expression of assuming a superior stance, and is quite likely to make the other person feel small.

Avoid personal references to your own experience

This is a difficult guideline for many people to understand. Surely sharing one's own experience helps to create a good personal relationship? After all, using good listening skills is not like psychoanalysis, where the analyst traditionally maintains anonymity. Yet directly sharing personal experience has its dangers. It draws attention away from the speaker's story towards the helper's story, and may even give rise to some envious admiration on the part of the person seeking help. 'My word, he got over a similar loss in six months: he must be a balanced person', thinks the person who has just learned that the helper too was bereaved recently. An even more cogent reason for avoiding personal references is that (as in using identification instead of empathy) the helper's experience, however similar it may appear, is not the same as the other's, and there are probably other dimensions to the other person's experience which were not present in that of the helper. It is presumptuous to think that any two people follow the same path through a common crisis, or that one person's solution is generally applicable.

In fact carers can and do use their own experiences much more than the person being helped ever needs to know. Every experience provides the starting-point for making good empathic responses, as long as the empathy is conveyed tentatively, constantly checking out that it seems accurate. If the helper has suffered a bereavement, whether or not it is similar to the other's loss, it is possible to draw upon aspects of that experience in trying to identify similarities between the situations, using skills already discussed in previous guidelines in this chapter.

Avoid burdening the person with your own difficulties

This guideline is a natural extension of the last. It does not help the speaker at all when the helper shares their own problems. To do so may even lead the speaker to imagine that, given the helper's circumstances, they should not be troubled any further. If helpers cannot put their personal issues to one side in an interview, they should not, for the time being, engage in their caring work. Nevertheless, if the helper is able to be more empathic by using their own difficulty to identify any similarities with the other person's circumstances, this may be very useful in the caring process – as long as the helper does not confuse self and other.

Avoid threats or pressure

The work settings of those who use caring skills, whether professionally or in a voluntary capacity, vary so greatly that it is dangerous to make sweeping generalizations about this guideline. A disciplinary matter in a work setting may require a warning – whereas threats or pressure are obviously inappropriate when a helper is listening to a person who is talking of suicide (because it is only meeting threat with threat). When a line manager has to switch from using listening and responding skills in a caring manner to engaging in a disciplinary hearing, it is not easy to be facilitative. Yet most people do not like having to discipline others, and might welcome alternative ways of dealing with such matters. One way, which requires more time perhaps, and the co-operation of the person who is being disciplined, is to concentrate much more on the obvious and underlying reasons for what has gone wrong, rather than on spelling out future sanctions if the offence is repeated. Some situations might have been averted had someone in a managerial role acted earlier. Distaste for taking up uncomfortable matters perhaps explains a general reluctance to address them when they are first noticed. 'I'll wait and see' is often a formula for hoping the problem will go away.

Listening and responding well is not a soft option. It is not only hard work – because so many unhelpful responses have to be restrained; it also requires a toughness which those who take up caring work frequently do not like to show. Counsellors and therapists learn to be firm on boundaries – of time, availability, and about payments, etc. Those who use counselling skills in their caring work similarly need to learn how to resist pressures, and to be firm where necessary with those who in one way or another play the helper along. Being firm does not mean using threats, but it might mean being completely open: 'I have made three appointments to see you already and you haven't turned up. If there is some difficulty, let's talk about it.'

Exercise 17

This exercise presents the reader with a number of statements, selected because they present the listener with some difficulty in knowing how best to respond. First think of an inappropriate response (one which clearly breaks any of the 'avoid' statements listed above). If you are working in small groups these responses should be shared, and the group should select the one that is the biggest howler. Having expressed a bad response, return to the original statement and consider what might be a good response, drawing on many of the types of response which have been discussed in this chapter. Each response can be shared in the small group, and the group can decide which might be the most appropriate reply to make. For example:

'I feel like sticking a knife in my wife.'

Some inappropriate responses: 'How dreadful!'
'That sounds very Freudian.'
'What stops you?'

Some appropriate responses: 'That sounds a frightening
feeling to have.'
'What makes you feel like doing
that?'
'You sometimes feel you'd like to
be rid of her?'

It is obviously impossible through the printed word to convey the way in which these remarks might be said. This should nevertheless be considered in this exercise, because some statements, which on paper appear to be inappropriate, may in fact be good responses – providing they are said in the right tone of voice. Even fairly hard and potentially threatening phrases can be said softly and with encouragement, to good effect. Likewise phrases which on paper appear appropriate may be said in a shocked or critical manner. The second of the appropriate responses above is a good example: said in a sharp tone it would be very judgemental. It is possible that the same phrase could therefore be used for both the appropriate and inappropriate response, differing only in the way it is expressed.

There is more to the first part of the exercise, the inappropriate response, than simply a bit of fun. If the helper can respond spontaneously inwardly, and acknowledge silently this immediate reaction, it can help identify any hidden agenda that could get in the way of making a more appropriate response. This period of self-reflection emphasizes the value of allowing a little pause before replying, to be sure that an unhelpful sentiment does not slip out, either in words or in tone of voice.

Suggest inappropriate and then appropriate responses for some or all of the following statements:

1. You don't understand.
2. I can't work with . . . (a colleague).
3. I can't stand men.
4. You're not helping me at all.
5. Can't you tell me what to do?
6. Do you like me?
7. I can't agree with your decision.
8. I'm wasting your time. There must be others with bigger problems than me.
9. When am I going to start feeling better?
10. I don't know how you can just sit there and listen to people moaning all day.

Exercise 18

Everyone experiences occasions in listening, in helping and in everyday conversations, when they regret the reply they gave to something they were told. Afterwards they think to themselves, 'If only I had said . . .'; or 'What on earth made me say that?'

If a number of people in caring positions, whether ministers or lay visitors, voluntary workers, teachers or managers, can get together regularly for about an hour (depending on the size of the group), an exercise which is similar to Exercise 17 can help them to refine their responses in and to awkward situations, or to difficult statements. Helpers and carers can build up a repertoire of ways of responding and, with experience, can learn from their mistakes. In such a group, members take it in turns to introduce the situation, *very* briefly; then they tell the other members what was said to them, and what they said in reply. The best learning comes from those situations where they felt they said completely the wrong thing. The original statement, spoken by the person seeking help, can then be repeated and each person in the group in turn can suggest in direct speech what they would say in response to those words. It is not necessary to enter into explanations – just speak the different responses in turn. Then the group can select which the majority think is the most appropriate response. When one member has shared a situation in this way, and heard alternative responses, the next member takes over, with a new statement from a new setting. Appointing a group facilitator each time may help to keep the different contributions moving, so that background information and explanation is minimized. The exercise concentrates on the responses to single statements, not on the whole situation – and it is important to give every member of the group a chance to participate.

Example of unfortunate response:

VISITOR	[*to a long-term elderly woman patient on a psychiatric ward*] And what do you do while you're in here?
ELDERLY PATIENT	Oh, I just knit all day.
VISITOR	I see. If I had to knit all day it would drive me mad![1]

14. Avoid changing the subject or interrupting unnecessarily

The various responses suggested in the guidelines in this chapter enable the helper to stay attentive to the person who is telling their story. This close, accurate tracking of what the speaker is saying does not demand a large number of responses. Anxious about what to say next, too many helpers seize on the first question that comes to mind, and ask it without thinking about whether it is connected to anything that has been said. This can be even more tempting if the subject which is being talked about or alluded to is one which might become upsetting, anxiety-provoking, or embarrassing.

Most people who want to talk to a helper say more than enough to enable the helper to select a relevant aspect to pursue, if this becomes necessary. One of the skills of active listening is to isolate what is important, and not to be sidetracked down irrelevant byways which take the speaker away from their central concern. If a major theme develops – and it often does in terms of a decision to be made or a feeling that needs to be more fully expressed – the helper should stay with it, allowing the speaker to elaborate as much as is necessary. It can also be helpful to draw together various references to a similar issue or set of feelings, and to link in variations with it, as is illustrated in Guideline 15 below.

Sometimes the person who is telling their story drifts away from what they were saying. This may be because something more important has arisen, which must be shared, but it is sometimes because in their distress they move into less relevant details or side-tracking. Here the listener may want to interrupt: 'Perhaps it's difficult because talking in this way makes you feel awful, but I felt you drifted away from what you were saying. Would you like to come back to it?' Another important occasion for interruption is when the listener is unclear about some factual point, or when the speaker makes a quick reference which it could be helpful to know a little more about. The danger of this latter reason for interrupting is that it stems the flow of the story; furthermore, if the speaker is expressing strong feelings, it might be better to let a detail pass, coming back to it later if the opportunity arises. Even a helpful interruption might lead to the speaker asking, 'Where was I?' A helper must therefore always be prepared to bring the story line back to where it was before the interruption, acknowledging their part in the diversion: 'I interrupted you just now, at the point when you were describing such and such. You may want to go back to that.'

15. Identify links between different experiences, events, reactions and ideas

The guidelines for listening and responding have up to now concentrated on what the person seeking help wishes to say, the different messages they are conveying in what they say, how they are feeling, and how the helper can most appropriately and accurately respond to what the speaker has expressed. The listener tries to help the speaker to hear what they have been saying and to share some of the feelings they appear to be experiencing. These basic skills are very important, and underpin any development to more advanced skills used in some interviewing and in much counselling. The person who has sought help is given an opportunity to see themselves and their problems in perspective, and by expressing themselves fully they often feel less distressed and more clear about the dimensions of the issue.

Yet the helper who listens carefully is in a position to do more than reflect back what they have heard and observed, as I have already shown in discussing the way in which empathy can be used to enable a person to get more in touch with their feelings. In listening empathically the carer listens to the inner self as well as to the speaker, and sometimes shares a possible feeling or mood which the speaker could be experiencing but has not yet recognized or not yet shared in the interview. The helper has therefore added something, which, it is hoped, fits what the person is experiencing, but which always needs to be checked out to see if the idea is valid. This guideline points to another way in which the listener may process what they are hearing, and considers whether this can be reflected back to the speaker. In this case it is more connected with what the listener *thinks* than with what the listener *feels*. The listener, being in a different position, is sometimes able to see aspects of a situation which the speaker has not yet fully grasped. When these aspects are put to them, the speaker might reply, 'I hadn't seen it that way. That's useful.'

Such observations are frequently made about similarities between the different parts of the story that is being told, and in contradictions and conflicts which the speaker has alluded to at various times in the interview, or over a series of interviews. An example of this is Del, who one week was talking to his helper about the way in which his father had reacted to his mistakes. Del's father had a way of picking up issues and saying, 'Why didn't you . . . ?' The next week Del was describing a social occasion when he had not been as good at chatting to the others present as he had wanted to be. He felt low afterwards, and he said to himself (in the identical tone of voice that he had used of his father), 'Why didn't I . . . ?' Del's helper pointed out how similar both these phrases were, even in the way in which Del had said them, and suggested that his father's voice seemed now to be inside him, especially when he felt he had failed in any of the tasks he set himself.

These types of observation are often so obvious to the listener that it is tempting to ignore them, because it seems that the person speaking must have seen the links themselves. But the helper will be responding usefully, even if the link is one which the speaker has already recognized, because to reflect it is a good empathic response, supporting the speaker's insight. If the speaker has not recognized the link, this kind of response can come like a bright ray of light in the darkness. For example, at the beginning of an interview, Kathy explained how low she had felt over the last six months. Only later did it come out that in December (and the listener quickly calculated that this was six months ago) Kathy had had a miscarriage. It may appear as obvious to the reader as it did to the helper that the onset of Kathy's depression coincided with her miscarriage. But it was not so obvious to Kathy, who replied, when the link to that time was made, 'I hadn't thought of that. I think I've tried to forget all about it.'

Sometimes the helper who is listening carefully picks up a contradiction in what the other person is saying – a contradiction which might indicate the presence of potential conflict of opposing feelings. At one point of an interview Susan talked very adoringly of her boyfriend, but some ten minutes later she described how intolerant she had been of him when he did not turn up one day, having promised her he would. Yet she had said nothing to him about it. The helper then reflected that Susan must have been feeling pretty angry, and had found it difficult to tell her boyfriend just what she felt. Perhaps she adored him so much that she was afraid telling him what she felt might distance them too greatly.

In counselling and psychotherapy these responses are known as interpretations or constructions. They depend on the helper putting together various ideas, and making a particular contribution which adds to what the speaker has expressed. There is a danger that the helper's interpretation will not be what the other person feels or thinks, which is why interpretations must be made carefully. In less formal counselling situations and in other helping interviews, these same links, and the clarification of conflicting feelings and pressures, frequently enable the person seeking help to see different dimensions of the issue, to look from another perspective or angle, and to make more sense of what is happening to them. These observations cannot be effectively made unless the helper listens well, and by careful responses enables the speaker to tell the story more fully, so providing a more accurate picture from which the helper can construct other ways of seeing.

Exercise 19

Because these kinds of link or interpretation are often made more extensively in a counselling interview, I set out below a summary of the main points expressed by a client, and the principal observations made by the counsellor, in a single session – the first of a number that took place. The session serves as an example in which the reader can observe the different links which can be made. The sequence of the session, the client and the counsellor speaking, is shown through the numbers attached to each section.

Read through the session and note down the connections which the counsellor appears to make. There are six such links (with the answers below), some of which are more obvious than others.

1.	STEVE	I'm in a muddle. A number of things have gone wrong, but they all stem from my girlfriend breaking off our relationship a month ago. People tell me it's only 'teenage love'. On the day my girlfriend walked out, I hitched down south to see my mother.
2.	COUNSELLOR	(*Thinks*: 'mother', not 'parents') [*paraphrases and empathizes*] The central thing that has gone wrong is the break with your girlfriend which appears to have taken you by surprise.
3.	STEVE	We've been living together for 18 months. I felt so mature and grown-up. We were going to get married, and buy a house [*Steve is eighteen*]. (A number of things had gone wrong before the break – a holiday with mother and girlfriend; running into a police car.)
4.	COUNSELLOR	Holiday? [*chooses the word 'holiday' as a minimal prompt rather than 'police car'*]
5.	STEVE	(Describes this holiday.) Also with us on the holiday was my mother's new boyfriend – a policeman. (Things went wrong after this.)
6.	COUNSELLOR	[*closed question*] When did your parents separate?
7.	STEVE	My mother left my father seven years ago: she just walked out. I lived with my father. (A lot of detail follows about the domestic life he and father had together. How father made sure he and Steve had a good home together.)
8.	COUNSELLOR	Perhaps one of the reasons *you* did not see your own relationship as 'teenage love' is because you and your girlfriend have become the couple your parents weren't, and you too have been creating a home.
9.	STEVE	I hadn't seen it that way, but it makes sense. But my girlfriend is not a substitute for my mother.

10. COUNSELLOR (*Thinks:* I'm not so sure; this may be part of it.)

11. STEVE (Talks more about his father, and how upset father was when mother got a boyfriend and moved out.) My girlfriend also got a new boyfriend.

12. COUNSELLOR And you feel upset just as you remember your father being upset?

13. STEVE [*Steve's eyes have been looking very moist during 11, and when the counsellor links father and himself he looks more tearful. There is a silence.*]

14. COUNSELLOR [*breaks silence*] Perhaps you are finding it difficult because you had felt so grown-up and mature. Now your girlfriend has left, you are really upset.

15. STEVE [*In response to 14 Steve now begins to cry.*] I feel silly crying in front of you. I never cry in front of people.

16. COUNSELLOR People tell you you're like a teenager, but you want to be grown-up, and you don't think grown-ups should cry?

17. STEVE Do you think I should see the doctor and have antidepressants?

18. COUNSELLOR [*alternative response to answering the question*] Grief is natural, although it is very painful. You are grieving because the bottom has dropped out of your world, and you feel confused.
[*The counsellor gives Steve a chance to dry his tears. Since it is near end of session the counsellor encourages him to become more settled, by talking about a few minor issues. They arrange a time to meet the next week.*]

The links

18 connects back to 1: Steve's 'I'm in a muddle' is picked up in the counsellor's phrase 'you feel confused'.

1 and 7: Steve uses the same phrase – 'walked out' – which the

counsellor uses to link Steve's situation and his parents' marriage breaking. But the counsellor is not yet ready to link mother and girl-friend as similar key figures in Steve's life.

1 is taken up in 8 and 16: Steve uses the phrase 'teenage love' in his opening story, and the counsellor gently alludes to this in an empathic reference to Steve not believing this to be 'teenage love' (8). Later the counsellor uses the reference in a different way, by helping Steve to recognize that although he does not believe he is just a teenager (and so doesn't want to look immature), adults also cry.

3 and 5: Steve makes two distinct references to the police. This may be accidental in more ways than Steve's reference to the police car, and the evidence is probably too circumstantial (!) at this point for the counsellor to do anything but note it. It may later turn out to have symbolic significance for Steve.

3 is taken up in 14 and 16: The counsellor makes use of Steve's earlier phrase about feeling 'grown-up/mature', to ease the way for Steve to show his less 'grown-up' feelings (as he will perceive them) and reassures him that this is all right in the further reference in 16 in using 'grown-up' rather than 'adult' – an interesting choice of word which appeals to Steve's worry about his maturity (it is a word we tend to use with children) without being condescending.

11 repeated in 12: Steve has almost made this link himself – he certainly uses his father's situation as a reflection of his own. The counsellor makes this rather more explicit, and introduces the feelings that are equally present in this historical link.

16. Avoid speaking too soon, too often, or for too long

WAIT

LISTEN

RESPOND   simply
           accurately
           to the point
           and keep it brief!

and then

LISTEN

Remember that the person who wants to tell their story has not come to see the helper in order to listen, and is probably so full of what is happening to them that they will only take in a little of what the helper says. The Law of Diminishing Returns applies: the more the helper says, the less the other person will hear.

17. Return to the listening mode, to watch and listen for the reaction to your own response, as well as for anything new that emerges

Any conversation or interview is a two-way process, with a constant shifting between listening and responding. In the caring situations addressed in this book, the helper devotes more time to listening than to responding. There is always a certain amount of tension for the helper, who is bound to wonder how to respond most appropriately to the other person's story and to any distress, and wonders when to do this. This tension may be temporarily relieved when the helper intervenes, and at this point, when the helper is speaking, they may find it more difficult to monitor the effect on the other person of what they are saying. It is important to try to do this, because the helper may express a particular aspect badly, and it may be obvious from the other person's facial response that the other has taken it the wrong way, for example critically; or it might be clear that the speaker has not understood what the helper is trying to say. The helper should look at the other person while the helper is responding, to try and perceive how their intervention is being taken. This is not as simple as it sounds, because many people prefer to look back and forth when they are speaking, even if when they listen they can more easily look at the other person. The relief of making a response can also lead to a temporary lapse of attention in the helper once a response has been given, although this may be the very point when either some misunderstanding or anxiety is present if the response was not well phrased; or when the other person makes a revealing response to a helpful intervention. Whether the helper has responded well or has missed the point, the reply to the helper's words takes the interview further.

And so it goes on, back and forth, swift to hear, slow to speak, swift to hear again. In summary, Guidelines 16 and 17 say it all. The helper listens, observes and monitors their own reactions, whether in thought or feeling. When it seems right, the helper responds, and then returns to attentive listening and observation. It seems so simple. Putting all the guidelines together is a little more complex, as the next chapter shows.

FOUR

Putting the Guidelines Together

Learning and practising each of the separate listening and responding skills is relatively straightforward. Putting them together in a single conversation or an interview, so that good listening is combined with making the most appropriate response, is rather more difficult. At first it seems impossible to remember it all, and old habits slip in (particularly the habit of asking many closed questions). Listening well and responding well takes a lot of practice, not only in the relative safety of a training course, but in 'real life' too.

The following two exercises provide ways of starting the practice of integrating these different skills. The first is a short trial run to initiate the skills of listening well, with the expectation that there will not be the need to make many interventions. The second exercise introduces a number of miniature role plays, and introduces a checklist (Figure 1) to help the listener to review their interventions. This record – along with Figure 2, introduced later in this chapter, which measures helper and client participation – can be used in the longer role plays that follow. These more complex role plays provide opportunities for practising the skills in relation to a number of different situations.

Exercise 20

The student group splits into small groups of three or four people. Each person takes their turn to be (a) the speaker, (b) the listener, and (c) one (or two) observers. There are therefore three or four subsections to the exercise, each lasting 20 minutes, which includes time for the group to discuss how much the listener's skills encouraged the speaker. The speaker selects any of the topics below and talks on that topic, while the listener tries to draw out the particular feelings suggested. Since this is a trial run, just 12 minutes are allowed for this conversation (one of the observers can keep the time), after which the observers share their comments; and the conversation is reviewed by everyone, for a further eight minutes. It is particularly important that the speaker chooses a topic which is not too painful to recall.

1. *Speaker*: Speak about your first real job, especially what it was like starting it in the first few days.
   Listener: Draw out the pleasant and the less pleasant features in the speaker's story.

2. *Speaker*: Speak about your memories of one of the schools you attended.
   Listener: Draw out what the speaker liked and disliked about being at school.

3. *Speaker:* Describe one person who has had a major influence on you, either on your ideas and beliefs, or on the pattern of your life.
   Listener: Draw out ways in which the person described has changed the speaker's ideas or path of their life.

When everyone has had their turn at each part of this exercise, discuss the ease or difficulty of listening, and what kind of interventions seemed to be most helpful to the speaker.

Exercise 21

The exercise is similar to Exercise 20, but in this case a recorder (one of the observers where there is a group of four), completes a checklist of the types of intervention which the helper makes in response to the person who is telling their story.

The checklist is reproduced in Figure 1. It consists of two sets of interventions: those which are generally felt to be facilitative, and those which are generally considered to be less helpful or even disruptive to the progress of a helping interview. There is space to list some of these less helpful or loaded remarks (see Guideline 13). The recorder ticks off one box for each intervention the helper makes. Sometimes it is difficult to be certain which category an intervention falls into (for example, a rhetorical question might also be a paraphrase or a minimal prompt). But these fine distinctions are not important; it is the overall impression that counts, and which can

Figure 1 Types of Intervention

Tick the relevant line each time the helper responds. If the whole row is used up, start again making ticks into Xs.

Allowing more than brief silence																	
Minimal prompt ("Yes . . .") (after client has spoken)																	
Reflecting back client's last words																	
Paraphrasing what client has said																	
Empathic response																	
Suggesting thought/feeling expressed non-verbally																	
Open question to prompt																	
Closed question to get information																	
'Why . . .' question																	
Question or remark that changes subject																	
Linking two or more references																	

Giving advice/instruction																	
Offering practical help																	
Talking about self not client																	
Gender/racial stereotyping																	
Offputting/loaded remarks by helper (specify below)																	

Offputting remarks:

Helper _____   Client _____   Recorder _____

prove useful feedback to the helper. Since this is a relatively short conversation, there may not be many interventions, but use of the checklist enables the participants to begin to master its categories for further use in role-play practice (Exercises 22 and 23).

Each person in the foursome has the opportunity of being the 'client', relating an early helping experience where they first felt they really helped someone (not necessarily through any sophisticated knowledge or skill on their part), and where a personal relationship was part of, or a consequence of, the helping. Just writing to someone would not be a good example. It may be helpful to have time to think about this in the week before the teaching session, if you are given prior warning of the topic.

The task of the helper in this exercise is a specific one: in addition to encouraging the person telling their story, they should draw out the different *feelings* which were experienced at the time of this early helping experience. Take it in turns to play the roles of the helper, the 'client' and the recorder (and where there are four participants, the observer). Each turn for this exercise lasts 20 minutes in all, with 12 minutes for the 'client' and helper to work together, and a further eight minutes for the group to review the intervention checklist and to consider other aspects of the helper's use of skills and the 'client's' experience of the exercise. The observer (if there is a fourth person) listens out for anything which the helper may have missed in the exploration of the original experience.

Exercise 22

Despite the fact that role play is in some ways artificial and contrived, it often gets very close to the real situations in which carers and helpers find themselves. Those who play the part either of the client/speaker or of the helper/listener frequently comment on the way in which either role becomes more real than they had imagined. This makes proper debriefing at the end of a role play essential.

Debriefing involves both 'client' and 'counsellor' or helper describing how they felt in the role they were playing. It helps the person playing the client to put these feelings into the third person: for example, if Jeff is playing a client called Richard, Jeff is encouraged to avoid saying, 'I felt better when the counsellor said . . .', and instead to say, 'Richard felt better . . .', reserving for his own comments the first-person pronoun: 'I thought you did very well, and could see how you helped Richard with this difficulty'. The person playing the counsellor or helper, since they nearly always play themselves, does not need to speak in the third person. It may also be important for each to be able to disown any part of the role which is particularly different from their real self or real role: for example, Jeff might say, 'I need to point out that I am not nearly as irritable as Richard'; and the helper may need to say, 'I am much more used to being a teacher engaged in pastoral care than a school counsellor, and so I found it difficult to work with the more formal aspects of the session'. Finally each person playing a role may need the chance to reinforce their own personality by taking a minute or two at the end of the discussion of the role play to remind everyone who they really are, and perhaps what they are going on to do next that day. Jeff may therefore say at the end of the debriefing and discussion of the role play: 'I am Jeff, not Richard, and I'm off home now to my partner and family, and I'm going to spend the evening watching television'. In order for the debriefing to take place, it is important that someone in each group (the observer), or the person conducting the role-play exercise, takes the lead in ensuring that the different aspects of debriefing are fully covered.

I introduce debriefing at this point as an essential part of the role-playing of the situations in Exercises 22–24. In the role plays that follow each person in a group of three or four has the opportunity to play a different 'client', and to be a 'counsellor', the recorder of the checklist (Figure 1) used in the previous exercise, and an observer (where there are four). If there is the additional observer, they can keep the time, and share observations during the debriefing period. There are three or four periods of 20 minutes in all, 12 minutes for each role play, and a further eight minutes for observer feedback and discussion in each role play, before changing round the positions which each person takes.

The following 'client' scripts provide opportunities for each person to take a different role for each period of the exercise. The helper can choose whether he or she wishes to be a counsellor, or to take some other caring role.

1. You are Jane or John, aged 20. You have come see the helper (an employer, youth leader or another adult you have known for a while) to ask for a reference. You are applying for a job in another town, and putting on a brave face about the idea

of moving away. You feel you have grown up and need to be independent of home. You are restless because two months ago you started to go steady with your partner. Although the family has no personal objection to this person, the whole business has given rise to family rows. Father rules the roost at home. He takes all the decisions. He has become involved in all your attempts to go out with your partner, because he complains about your returning home late, even if it is only a few minutes late. He has been staying up to see you in, and he questions you about where you've been. There are even rows on occasions when you want to go out. Your mother simply falls in with what father says, saying that he is right, and that he is only protecting you for your own good.

2. You are Mr (or Mrs) Smith, and the helper has called on your mother, who lives with you, and who has not been to the day centre for a few weeks. Your mother, Mrs Edwards, has in fact been staying with your brother for the last week. She gives the impression to others that she is a sweet, if rather vague, old person – but your experience of her at home is that she can be very awkward. Three weeks ago she got on your nerves so much that you were rather rough with her, both in what you said and physically. You regretted it immediately, and you found an excuse each time to prevent your mother from going to the centre, in case she said something. You are afraid that you may snap again. You find it difficult at first to admit anything more than that your mother is awkward; but if the helper is empathic, and you trust them, you will be able to admit that you lost your temper, and to ask for some help with the situation.

3. You are Lesley or Leslie, well-educated, respectable, and rather 'proper', a pillar-of-the-church type, on the church council, and looking to become a churchwarden. You have been married for 17 years and have two teenagers, who are much more laid back than you – and they have obviously been enjoying life to the full. Your marriage has always been secure and stable, but perhaps (in the light of recent events) it has been rather conventional and dull. Your partner is not interested in the church. You have fallen for another church

member who sings in the choir, and who you thought was similarly 'upright'. You met because you belong to the same house group, and this person asked for a lift home at the end of the evening. In talking to this person you discovered how much you have in common, and you have fallen in love. You feel young again. You have come to see someone you trust because the feelings are so strong you don't know how to handle them. You feel the only decent thing to do is to tell your partner, and perhaps arrange a trial separation without any fuss or hard feelings; and you want someone to tell you that this is a good idea.

4. You are Dean or Tracy. You left school when you were 16 and have been at work a few weeks. At the youth club one evening some of your friends were discussing work, and you said you did not feel stretched by your job. Someone said you should get a better one, but you replied you did not have proper qualifications. You lack confidence in yourself, and you show this by the way in which you dismiss suggestions which might help you to get a better job – a college course, qualifications, training and similar ideas your helper may put to you. You come from a good home, and your father is a very successful businessman, sure of himself, always giving advice and expressing sound opinions. Your elder brother, Mark, did well at school and is a chartered accountant. Mother is very proud of the family and the home, and boasts how clever you both are, even though you do not feel it. She tends to fuss around you and treat you still as the baby of the family. Father wanted you to leave school at 16 (your results were not good) and to stand on your own feet.

5. You are Mrs Fisher, and you approach your helper to talk about your son Jim, who is 15 and a real tearaway: he is virtually uncontrollable at home; he stays out late; he is not working at school, and even gets into trouble there. He has been this way for over 12 months, since his Dad died. You can elaborate on Jim's problems and the difficulties you have handling him. But although Jim is difficult, that is only half your story. If the helper gives you the opportunity, you can talk about the death of your husband; how he was a very hard-working

man, who did much overtime, and of whom you saw little; even at weekends he went fishing on his own. So you did not have much of a relationship with his father, nor did Jim, and he was not much help in bringing the family up. You resent and miss your husband, who, for all his distance, did seem to have some stabilizing effect on Jim.

6.   You play Annie, a widow and a pensioner, and you are in hospital for the removal of your gall-bladder. The operation was successful, but you have just learned that your grandson was operated on in the same hospital for injuries received in an accident and did not recover consciousness. You lost another grandson 18 years ago, and 12 years ago your husband died. Your own mother died 18 months ago after you had nursed her for a very long time. Your only son died a year ago, and your father died when you were a child. But you have sustained through all this a simple, primitive faith, that these things were meant to happen, and it was your lot in life. The Lord has seen you through; it must be his will, it must be what he wants for you. You have been through a lot, and living by faith you will be able to go through much more. If you need help at all, it is in having someone who understands everything that has happened to you, including your profound faith.

7.   You are James, a 30-year-old man, married with no family, a clerk in a solicitor's office. You are, and always have been, an active server at your local church, and you were educated at public school. You are soaked in your faith. You are very particular that everything should be done the right way, at home, in the office, and in church; and you are therefore very thorough in your own preparation for receiving communion – confession each month, sometimes more often. You approach your priest to ask his advice. You like a quick drink before going to bed, and an occasional drink at dinner parties, but you are by no means a heavy drinker. It relaxes you, and makes you feel less anxious. But you are none the less anxious that this is the beginning of the slippery slope; you feel you ought not to receive communion when you have had a drink the night before. You want to know whether this is right, and

you need your priest to give you a definitive answer. But should you get such an answer you are not able to stay happy with it for long. 'But', you might say, 'I am afraid of the drinking getting out of control'; or, 'But I do like a drink because it calms me down', etc. You are one of life's worriers! There is a 'but' for every reassuring word.

Exercise 23

In this exercise there are more complex role-play scripts, which enable you to practise for considerably longer. For these role plays it is helpful to use 'time-out' (explained below), together with a time-record sheet which helps track the degree to which the helper can allow the other person to speak, and permit silences, as well as keeping a running total of the amount of time out taken.

This role-play exercise is better done in groups of six or seven, in which there is the main speaker, the listener, two people to record interventions and time, and two or three observers. One of the recorders uses the checklist (Figure 1) introduced in Exercise 21. The second uses the time-sheet (Figure 2). Each box represents 30 seconds, and the time-keeper records whether each 30 seconds was used by the main speaker (here called 'client'), the helper, or whether silence or time out principally occupied the half-minute. Both these checklists can be referred to during time out, to assist the helper monitor their performance; and they can be given to the helper during the debriefing, as a record.

Time-out is an important feature of role-play work, greatly increasing the value of the role play for all the participants, whether the helper, the 'client' or the observers. In role-play work without time-out there is an additional strain for the person playing the helper, knowing that they are being watched, and with no chance of feedback or assistance from the observers until it is too late, in the debriefing at the end. The observers themselves may be itching to intervene, to say how they would meet the situation, but without a time-out they are frustrated and have to keep silent until the final discussion.

'Time-out' means that the listener or helper is less isolated, because he or she can ask, at any point and as many times as necessary, for time-out to consult with the observers, and to check on the progress of the listening and responding through the intervention

Figure 2 Measurement of Helper/Client Verbal Participation

Each box represents 30 seconds. If the time is filled mainly by the **Client**, mark 'C' in the box; if by the **Helper 'H'**; if it is mainly **silence**, mark 'S'. For '**Time Out**', mark 'T'.

Mins	1		2		3		4		5		6		7		8		9		10		Cs	Hs	Ss	Ts
0–10																								
11–20																								
21–30																								
31–40																								
																				TOTALS			

Helper _____ Client _____ Time-keeper _____

The role-play session lasts 40 minutes. Time-out can be taken as many times as the helper wishes, as long as the total time-out does not exceed 20 minutes (forty Ts). At the end of each line (ten minute period) the time-keeper should subtotal the time out.

record form (Figure 1) and the time-record form (Figure 2). Everyone except the 'client', who leaves the group during time out, can reflect upon progress so far; and can frame interventions that might be tried out when the 'client' comes back to continue the role play. During the time-out, when the 'client' leaves the group, he or she may be able to share the experience with 'clients' from other groups who are out at the same time.

When setting up the role play the tutor should suggest, or the group agree, how much of the allotted time for the whole role play can be given to time out. Thus it is possible, in the early stages of role-play work, to work to 20 minutes for the role play, with five minutes (or more) time-out allowed, and 20 minutes to debrief and discuss the work. Later a role play may last 40 minutes, with up to 20 minutes time-out allowed, or even 40 minutes with ten minutes time-out allowed, as participants become more experienced. In this case at least 20 minutes, perhaps more, might be given to debriefing and discussion – depending to some extent on the size of the role-play group (see below). It should be noted that the only person who can call time out is the helper – not the client, and not the observers – although a sensitive helper may recognize that it could be useful for the client too to have a time-out, as well as giving the helper the opportunity to review the work so far.

By using a time-out the person playing the helper invites the co-operation of the observers. Instead of waiting throughout to say what they would do, they have a responsibility to support the helper, and prepare them for the return of the client. Unhelpful competitiveness is thereby reduced. The observers are alert during the role play, not knowing any more than the helper, because they may be asked not just for feedback on the work, but also for an opinion on what to do or say. In making their suggestions they are putting themselves on the line as well, encouraging co-operative working. Sometimes in the first time-out both helper and observers have ideas on how they would like to help, but do not know how to put those ideas into practice. It may take several times-out before the right response comes, and the helper progresses.

The helper should not feel that it is an admission of failure to call time out. Battling on, making little or no progress, is frustrating for everybody, including the client and the observers. If the helper does not use much time out, the penalty is that the role play, with the client present, goes on for a greater proportion of the time allotted!

The wise helper is not ashamed to ask for assistance and support. They may use a time-out as often and for as long as they like within the agreed limit. The time recorder can keep the helper informed about how much time is left.

It might also be useful to watch what happens during a time-out. When the group is more used to working in this way, there might even be an observer looking at the time-out process alone, commenting on how the observers set about trying to assist the helper. For example, do the observers bombard the helper with suggestions, trying to solve the problem, but not really assisting the development of good listening and responding skills?

Each situation in the role plays in this exercise is introduced with a brief for the helper/listener, which the observers and recorders should also know. Only the person playing the client should know what is in the client script. The debriefing which follows the role play is just as essential a part of the exercise as in Exercise 22, where debriefing is explained. Only when both (or all) the participants have had the opportunity to become themselves again should the group examine the finer details of the exercise, and in particular the helper's part in it. Remember that the person who played the client must be addressed by their real name, and should use the third person to speak of the experience of being the client. If these precautions are not followed, it is possible for someone to go on carrying the client role long after the role play and discussion period has finished. In these longer role plays the debriefing and discussion requires at least 20 minutes, since it also includes analysis of how the role play went, and what was particularly helpful or unhelpful in the way the counsellor or other listener handled the situation. One of the observers can facilitate the debriefing by ensuring that all aspects of the process are followed – that is, the sharing of the two record forms and the discussion.

Role play 1 Hazel

Brief for the helper: You are a schoolteacher, and Hazel is one of your students, aged 15. You can play this as not knowing her very well, having just started to teach her. One day she asks to see you, and you meet her at lunchtime.

Brief for Hazel: You are a 15-year-old student at a comprehensive school. You ask one of your teachers if you can meet, and you arrange to see the teacher one lunchtime. You start by saying that you are concerned about your best friend who has got into 'bad company' and is 'taking drugs' – you mean smoking pot. Your friend does not know that you are talking about her, so you are very concerned about confidentiality. You are also very concerned about what you can do for her, what help you can advise her to seek. You avoid, with anxiety or even anger, attempts by your teacher to find out about you, saying things like: 'It's my friend. Please help me to help my friend.'

You can also say that this friend's boyfriend has just moved into the neighbourhood. His parents are often away at weekends and he invites friends round to parties. Some of them are his cronies from another part of town, though some are also pupils at your school. They smoke joints, and your friend has had a smoke and it made her feel 'funny'. There is also pressure for sex, though she has avoided it so far.

In fact, this friend you start by talking about is really yourself. If your helper helps you feel confident in them, you may reveal this. But if it is directly suggested that you are the person, you can respond to this by owning it, as long as it is not too soon after you have started talking. You may react with a sense of shame and horror at being found out. You are scared of your parents' reaction if they knew, of the risk of police raids (however unlikely this really is), and of the pressure for sex.

Role play 2: Fran Black

Brief for the helper: You play someone who knows Ms Black's son Matt – perhaps a youth worker, a minister, a teacher. Fran Black has asked if she can talk to you, and she starts by telling you how Matt is getting on at university, where he went last October. It is now his second term, and you yourself have not seen him since he went to university.

Brief for Fran Black: Your only child Matt went up to university six months ago. You have made a time to speak to his former teacher, or youth club leader, or minister (decide this with the person playing the helper before you start). You start by saying what a good boy Matt is, how you expect great things of him, how you remember his childhood with pride, how hard he works, how kind he is to you and your husband, etc. Fill this out as much as you wish with what other people have said about him – his teachers, friends, etc.

In fact you are very worried, and if you feel that the helper gives you confidence to reveal your fears, you do so – although remember that you are afraid of facing the idea of 'failure'. Does the helper enable you to acknowledge that things might not be so good after all? If he or she does, you can tell the helper how Matt's phonecalls got fewer and fewer in the first term; how he was different over Christmas; how he gave up going to church with you; how he talked of being fed up, and mentioned others who had left university. You are afraid that he is now going to throw away all those years of education and leave. Your husband is not really interested, and when you try to talk to him about it he says that it is up to Matt.

Role play 3 Mr Clarke

Brief for the helper: You are a street warden (perhaps part of a Neighbourhood Watch scheme or a church representative) and you know that Mrs Clarke has recently died. You visit Mr Clarke, although you do not know him very well because he has tended to keep himself to himself.

Brief for Mr Clarke: You are in your early sixties, recently bereaved; your wife Betty died after a long illness during which she was at home. You are extremely sad, and speak very slowly. There are many silences if your helper allows them. You speak of how good Betty was to you – 'one of the best'. You were married for 39 years, and if she had lived until Easter you would have celebrated your Ruby Wedding. She had been such a good patient. You retired early to look after her... and now this... You wish you could join her. Nothing matters any more.

If the visitor makes it possible, you can reveal that the last few years have not been so good. Betty's illness made her very difficult to live with. There were arguments, she was awkward, and often you wished she would die... and now she has. The grief is compounded by guilt.

Role play 4 Len Davis

Brief for the helper: You are the local minister visiting one of the families in your congregation; they have recently moved into the area. The minister of their previous church commended them to you, but so far only Mrs Davis (Liz) and her aged mother have attended. When you call, Len Davis is the only one who is at home. You have not met him before.

Brief for Len Davis: You are in your mid fifties, and you and your wife Liz have just moved into the area in order to purchase a house large enough to have Liz's mother to live with you. Since it is your new minister who calls on you, you are careful what you say, especially at first. There are urgent jobs to do around the house, which means you cannot spare time for church at present, although you always attended regularly in the area where you lived before. It was very good of Liz to offer to have her mother at home, fulfilling her Christian duty. 'Honour your father and mother, etc.'

In fact, since your mother-in-law moved in you have welcomed every opportunity to get away from her incessant talking. You happily drop your wife and her mother off at church and return home for some peace and quiet. You are already aware of the tensions arising between the three of you. If the minister helps you to, express some of your feelings – your anger, your resentment, your wish to enjoy life now the children have left home, but also perhaps your guilt for feeling this way; then you can express more of your true self and allow yourself to drop the mask of being a 'good Christian'.

Role play 5 Neena

Brief for the helper: Before you start, agree with the person playing Neena what sort of helper it would be most appropriate and comfortable for you to play (a counsellor, teacher, doctor, etc.) and where the interview is taking place. You simply know her name is Neena, that she is an Asian teenager and that she is about 15 years old.

Brief for Neena: Before starting the interview, agree with your helper whether he or she is a teacher, counsellor, doctor, or someone else you might see. The helper only knows your name and approximate age (15 years). The information that follows is for you to share as and when it feels right to do so, and depending on how sensitive your helper is.

You moved into the area about ten weeks ago, and you are getting on well with a new group of friends. You start your interview by asking the helper a direct question, to which you would like a direct answer: 'Is it dangerous to go on the Pill?' You want an answer, although if your helper is encouraging, you are prepared to talk more widely about the background to your question. If your helper is either heavy-handed and moralistic, or more interested in giving you information than in the reasons for your question, or does not appear to understand the issues you face in your culture, you keep pressing for a clear answer.

Your question reveals that you like to have some clear idea of 'rules' for living, and you are actually concerned at first about whether the Pill is dangerous. But the real danger is what your parents would say if they found out, because they are both rather rigid people, with traditional Asian values; they are not so strict that you could really rebel against them, but you do feel a sense of frustration that they always tell you what is best for you, and always assume they are right. You have had to push them to allow you out more in the evenings with a group of Asian girlfriends, and this has begun to introduce you to all sorts of exciting possibilities. You do not yet have a boyfriend, although you are mixing in the group with young Asian men. But you are torn between what your parents would say and what the youth culture around you is saying – between being careful, and living in a way that seems to you a little dangerous. In all this it is not easy to get away from your need to have an adult tell you what is right and wrong.

Role play 6 *Hannah or Ben*

Brief for the counsellor: This is a role play to practise more formal counselling, and should last the full 40 minutes. Your client is a 26-year-old man (Ben) or woman (Hannah). This is a second session. In the first he or she mainly communicated the information given below. At the end of the first session it was agreed that you would meet for eight sessions with the focus of helping the client to tell the family about his or her relationship – and the client agreed that they must be told soon, since he or she realized there was no point delaying, and that delaying might further endanger the relationship.

The story is as follows: he or she has lived with a non-Jewish partner for two years and has kept the relationship secret from his or her Jewish family: they have always assumed he or she would marry a Jew, as have the elder brother and sister. This is very important to the parents. The client is the youngest by eight years, and both siblings have good careers and 'suitable' marriages. The partner is now very fed up and insisting that the client tell the parents about the relationship, and make a clear commitment if he or she wants the relationship to continue. At present the client arranges the relationship so he or she is always available to attend frequent family functions: the client cannot say 'No' to the family, although is doing so indirectly by being in this relationship. He or she is also indirectly always saying 'No' to the partner by the constant availability to the family.

The client has never openly opposed the family. He or she was a very protected child, watched over by parents, older siblings and grandparents, never allowed to ride a bike in case he or she got hurt; and as a teenager rarely allowed to use public transport, and a very close watch was kept on him or her. As the client got older he or she felt very controlled by this, but open opposition meant that mother cried and father became angry at her being upset. The present relationship has been a secret bid for freedom. The client presents pleasantly and reasonably, yet clearly avoids open conflict with anyone at all costs, although the current situation means that this option is no longer available.

Brief for Hannah or Ben: You are a 26-year-old man (Ben) or woman (Hannah) who has come for counselling. This is a second session. In the first you mainly told the counsellor the information given in the first two paragraphs below. At the end of the first session it was agreed that you would meet for eight sessions with the focus of helping you to tell your family about your relationship – and you agreed that they must be told soon: you realized there was no point delaying, and that delay might further endanger your relationship.

Your story is as follows: you have lived with a non-Jewish partner for two years and have kept the relationship secret from your Jewish family. They have always assumed you would marry a Jew, as have your elder brother and sister. This is very important to your parents. You are the youngest by eight years, and both siblings have good careers and 'suitable' marriages. Your partner is now very fed up and insists that you tell your parents about the relationship, and make a clear commitment if you want the relationship to continue. At present you arrange your relationship so you are always available to attend frequent family functions: you cannot say 'No' to your family, although you are doing so indirectly by being in this relationship. You are also indirectly always saying 'No' to your partner by your constant availability to your family.

You have never openly opposed your family. You were a very protected child, watched over by parents, older siblings and grandparents. You were never allowed to ride a bike in case you hurt yourself; as a teenager you were rarely allowed to use public transport, and a very close watch was kept on you. As you got older you felt very controlled by this, but open opposition meant your mother cried and your father became angry with you for upsetting her. Your present relationship has been a secret bid for freedom. You always appear pleasant and reasonable and avoid open conflict with anyone at all costs, although the current situation means that this option is no longer available to you.

You start the second session from this position: although you decided in the first session to tell your parents, this leaves you feeling both frightened and furious. You continue to present pleasantly to the counsellor and appear to respond well (as you have learnt to do in your family). However this covers a passive hostility and anger which may come through if your counsellor tries to help you move forward on the course of action you have decided on. On the one hand, this is what you are asking the counsellor to help you with; but on the other, making any move means facing conflict, which is just what you always avoid. A part of you knows perfectly well that you cannot continue to run your life on this basis.

In this session you might use expressions like: 'I do see what you mean, but . . .'; 'That is a very good idea but it wouldn't work like that in my family'; 'It's so hard to explain, but saying things like that to my mother/father/partner just wouldn't work somehow'. Alternatively you might appear to agree readily to what is said, but it becomes apparent that this is not the case. You could become more openly hostile if the counsellor persists in trying to help you to make moves to tell your family, or begins to try to get you to look at what you are doing, and how you are responding etc., in the session. You are, however, very good at couching hostility in pleasantries. You could also refer to the counsellor perhaps not quite understanding the Jewish culture (nicely of course!).

You have a real difficulty in being autonomous, or in being

openly angry, and a real fear of both. If your counsellor is able to understand this empathically and help you to look at this, you may be able to respond, but remember that passive hostility will run deep.

Role play 7 Toni or Tony

Brief for the counsellor: This is a role play to practise more formal counselling, and should last the full 40 minutes. It is your first session with the client Toni or Tony, although the client has been seen for an assessment already in your counselling service, and from this assessment you know the following information.

The client is 22 years old. A year ago he or she was in a riding accident, hitting his or her head on a tree, being thrown from the horse, and then trampled on by the horse. As a result he or she suffered head injuries and serious injuries to the hip – a bone was crushed. He or she was in hospital for three months, in a wheelchair for another three, and although he or she can now walk, is limping and still experiences some pain. However, the client was optimistic in the assessment that in the long term mobility will be fully recovered – the doctors feel this is 90 per cent likely.

However, other injuries are also causing the client great distress: the sight in one eye was lost and will never be recovered; the hearing was damaged and is worsening – doctors have said that they cannot yet predict how bad this might become. Toni or Tony is a final-year law student wanting to go on to further training in law school and has always aimed to be a barrister specializing in civil rights. There are two older siblings: a brother who is a social worker, and a sister who is a doctor. The family is very supportive, and he or she is close to them; prior to the accident the client had been enjoying independence – after leaving school he or she had spent a year working abroad. The recent enforced dependence has been difficult, and this has been openly and honestly acknowledged within the family.

Since returning to university Toni or Tony has had to readjust to university life with a different group of students – since other friends had all graduated and left. This is what the client was finding difficult and so arranged to see a counsellor to talk about how it feels to return to university.

Brief for Toni or Tony: You are 22 years old. A year ago you were in a riding accident: you hit your head on a tree, were thrown from your horse, and the horse then trampled on you. As a result you suffered head injuries and serious injuries to your hip – a bone was crushed. You were in hospital for three months, in a wheelchair for another three, and although you can now walk, you are limping and still experience some pain. However, you are optimistic that in the long term your mobility will be fully recovered – the doctors feel this is 90 per cent likely.

However, other injuries are causing you the greatest distress: you lost the sight in one eye and this will never be recovered; your hearing was damaged and is worsening – doctors have told you that they cannot yet predict how bad this might become. You are a final-year law student wanting to go on to further training in law school and your aim has always been to be a barrister specializing in civil rights. You have two older siblings: a brother who is a social worker, and a sister who is a doctor. Your family is very supportive, and you are close to them; prior to the accident you had been enjoying your independence – after leaving school you spent a year working abroad. Your recent enforced dependence has been difficult for you, and this has been openly and honestly acknowledged within your family.

Since your return to university you have had to readjust to university life with a different group of students – since your friends have all graduated and left. This is what you have found difficult and you have arranged to see a counsellor to talk about how it feels to return to university. You were given an assessment at the counselling service, and are due to meet your actual counsellor for the first time. Everything above was talked about in the assessment, and your counsellor knows it too. But after the assessment you began to realize how devastated you feel by all that has happened to you. Your way of coping has been to believe firmly that you can overcome all this, and you have steered strongly away from what worries you most – the loss of hearing. It is this you are most defended against, and you have always refused to recognize this as a problem. On the morning of the day of your first appointment with the counsellor, you have received a letter saying that you have not been offered a place at law school. You are devastated and assume it is because of your hearing difficulties which you have always feared.

Role play 8 Peter or Petra
Brief for the counsellor: This is a role play to practise more formal counselling, and should last the full 40 minutes. The client has been

seeing you for six months in your capacity as a counsellor working in the local counselling centre. You have the same information in the next paragraph as the client has in her or his brief. This role play *starts* with a time-out so that you can brief the observer(s) about it, and work out how to handle a situation, *which your client does not yet know about.* The situation is that you are due to go on holiday in four weeks' time for a fortnight. You are aware that the only thing that keeps Peter or Petra going is this weekly session with you, which he or she has attended faithfully since you started. There is an additional factor in this role play, that if you take further times-out, each time you call the client back you must assume that it is the next session: so it is then *three* weeks before you go on holiday, then *two* weeks, etc. The client has also been briefed that it will be one week further on each time following a second or third time-out.

Peter or Petra came to see you six months ago because he or she was (and still is) depressed, and got (and gets) panic attacks whenever demands are made upon her or him with which the client feels he or she cannot cope. These sometimes happen at the office where the client has a job as a clerical assistant. The client's partner left two years ago. Peter or Petra has two teenage children, both of whom are due to leave home in a few weeks' time: one to go to college, the other to a job in another part of the country. They have been their parent's mainstay since the partner left. Although you (the counsellor) have also become a lifeline over these last few months, Peter or Petra is hardly any better than when he or she first came.

Brief for Peter or Petra: You have been seeing your counsellor for six months in the local counselling centre. The counsellor has been given all the information in the next paragraph before the role play starts, so you can assume that it is shared knowledge. This role play starts with a time-out (when you are absent from the group) so that the counsellor can brief the observer(s). In this role play, after each further time-out taken, you must assume that you are coming back to the next session one week later.

You came for counselling because you were (and still are) depressed, and you got (and get) panic attacks whenever demands are made upon you with which you feel you cannot cope. These sometimes happen at the office where you have a job as a clerical assistant. Your partner left you two years ago. You have two teenage children, both of whom are due to leave home in a few weeks' time:

one to go to college, the other to a job in another part of the country. They have been your mainstay since your partner left. Although
your counsellor has also become a lifeline over these last few
months, you are hardly any better than when you first came.

You will need to convey in this role play that your counsellor is
the only person you can really talk to, and the only person you feel
safe with. You can, of course, say this. You also keep asking questions
like, 'What's the matter with me? Will I get any better?' – although
try to avoid questions about what you should *do*. When the counsellor says things, try and convey how grateful you are for everything he or she gives you – how helpful the counsellor's remarks
are, how you hadn't seen things like that before, etc. In other words,
you are demanding but also dependent, hanging on every word. You
may come across therefore as quite agitated. Perhaps you only calm
down and become more genuinely constructive if your counsellor
can contain your feelings without panicking; and particularly if he
or she is able to help you get in touch with your anger at everyone
(including the counsellor) for leaving you so much of the time to
cope with things on your own.

Exercise 24

This exercise (called 'Storm over the breakfast table') provides a
larger group with the simultaneous experience of different role
plays, which are connected since they all relate to different family
members. It is particularly suitable as an ice-breaker or refresher
exercise when starting with a group which is already familiar with
the basic skills of listening and responding. It provides some
experience of the techniques used in psychodrama, and illustrates
the complexities of counselling only one person, when that person
often represents the dynamics within a couple, family or close
group, and suggests what might be involved in working with a
whole family. The exercise can take two or more hours if the group
is using all the possibilities suggested.

The following stages can be used in this exercise. Although they
might be omitted, Stages 11 and 13 are for use should the time available merit it.

Stages

1. Depending on the numbers in the group, there can be four or

five main characters. Having a fifth (David) introduces the need for another counsellor, assistant, timekeeper, etc. The exercise works best with four characters where there are up to 24 people in the group. Where there are more, the character of David enables more people to play an active part. Smaller groups need not include timekeepers, or *alter egos* (roles explained below). References to 'four or five' below depend upon whether the character of David is included, or is left as an absent member of the family.

2. Volunteers are needed or selected for the following roles: four or five to be the helpers, and four or five to be their assistants (for the initial briefing, time-out and debriefing). These counsellors and assistants are asked to leave the room after they have been given their briefing sheet; they are called back at the appropriate time.

3. A short summary of the Jones family situation is explained to everyone who is left.

4. Volunteers are needed or selected for the following roles: four or five to be the family members; if numbers permit, four or five to be each family member's *alter ego* (see below); four or five to be timekeepers during the different stages of the role play. Any people left over become observers.

5. The role of the *alter ego* is to act as the inner voice of the family member, assisting the person to get into the role; an *alter ego* also adds other dimensions to what the person might be experiencing; watches the breakfast scene and conveys other feelings the person may have before the counselling/helping session and during time-out; acts as a go-between in Stage 11, if time permits; and in the final dinner scene quietly prompts the family member with thoughts which might or might not be expressed.

6. Each family member, with her or his *alter ego*, is given five minutes to read through their individual roles (see briefs below) and discuss together how the family member may play their part.

7. Meanwhile, a table and five chairs are set around the table

(one chair stays empty whether four or five parts are played); and each timekeeper is asked to set up a small group of chairs elsewhere in the room, ready for the counselling/helping session to which they will be attached. Each timekeeper is assigned to a family member, and will be responsible for ensuring that, when the helping/counselling begins, the family member, the counsellor/helper, the *alter ego* and the counsellor's assistant are brought together as follows:

    (a) Brenda and the form tutor;
    (b) Mary Jones and the volunteer counsellor;
    (c) Bill Jones and his personnel manager;
    (d) Grandma Williams and the district nurse;
    (e) (David and the student counsellor).

8. The breakfast scene with the four family members is enacted for as long as any two members of the family stay round the table, or until enough heat has been generated! (David, if taking part in this exercise, watches from the sidelines.)

9. The helpers are called in, with their assistants. Timekeepers guide them to their 'corners'. The separate role plays start together and last for 30 minutes, including up to 15 minutes time-out. During times-out the family member and the *alter ego* leave, and only the assistant speaks to the helper, while any others observe.

10. Following the role plays, the helpers and their assistants once more leave the room, so that their assistants can help debrief the counsellors.

11. If there is time, there can now be a period of negotiation when any family member, through their *alter egos* acting as go-betweens, can contact any other family member to ask for a chat. If the family member approached does not wish to talk to that person, then she or he sends a message back through the *alter ego*. There can be as many changes of pairing during this period (up to 15 minutes) as necessary, before dinner is called.

12. The family members (less David, whether there are four or five parts) sit round the table for dinner that evening. They

resume relations as they wish. Call this scene to an end when enough has been said to illustrate either the success, or the failure, or the complexities, of the effects of the helping sessions. During this scene each *alter ego* sits behind and beside the appropriate family member, whispering prompts that might give expression to what that family member is thinking but is not yet saying.

13. If there is time, the helpers, with their assistants as *alter egos*, can then be asked to re-enact the scene at the breakfast table that morning as they imagine it, playing the character whom they helped, and drawing upon what they learned in the counselling interview as their script. It is interesting to refrain from indicating to them who sat where, and to see how the seating arrangements work out. (David's helper, if these roles were used, does not join in this.)

14. Debriefing of the family members, their *alter egos*, and eventually of the whole exercise must be done thoroughly in small groups – perhaps in the same groups as formed for the role plays. (See debriefing instructions in Exercise 22.) It is essential that the family members are thoroughly debriefed, and that there is some follow-up in the next session to check whether they have really left the role behind them. Simple though this preliminary situation is – apparently just a storm at a breakfast table – this exercise sometimes generates very strong feelings, and there is always the danger that family members continue to be identified by the class as 'Brenda', 'Mary', 'Bill' or 'Grandma', particularly if they have allowed their angry feelings to come through.

The exercise starts with the group setting up breakfast for the Jones family, with five chairs round a table (one represents the son's place, although he is away). The family lives in the suburbs of a large city: they are a typical family of four, with Mary Jones's mother (Mrs Williams) living with them. Mary and Bill have a son and daughter: David is away studying economics in London; Brenda is 15 and still at school. Bill works as a maintenance engineer on various widely scattered sites, and is constantly called out for emergency repairs; so home for him is a place to find some peace and quiet. Trouble is brewing. Brenda has dropped hints that she wants to do a paper round, which Mary Jones does not approve of: her exams come first. Grandma Williams does approve – she left school at 13 and it never did her any harm. Bill would just like some peace and quiet. It is breakfast time on a typical school day; everyone is up because it's shopping day for Mary, Grandma is expecting the district nurse, and Bill hasn't got to go in quite so early and so can offer Brenda a lift to school ...

Following an improvised scene at breakfast, four family members each seek some counselling from an appropriate helper. After these separate but simultaneous role plays the family members have the chance to talk with each other, in pairs and again at the evening meal. It is possible, as part of the debriefing, for the counsellors to take their clients' roles as they imagine them to have been at the original breakfast scene. Different stages in the exercise can be omitted where time is short. The exercise probably requires a large space or at least four small rooms.

Brief for the helpers and their assistants: There are four (or five) helpers, and, if numbers permit, each can have an assistant with whom to discuss the situation during times-out, which can be taken as usual. There may be others observing you, although only the assistant is permitted to comment during times out, since the other observers present will have watched the original scene. You leave the room while a family breakfast takes place in the Jones household. After breakfast, some time during that day, each member of the family has the chance of talking over their feelings with one of the helpers as follows: Mary Jones goes shopping in town, and calls at the local drop-in counselling centre where she talks to one of the volunteer counsellors. Bill Jones goes to work, and takes the opportunity of bringing up the situation with the personnel manager, to whom he goes to talk over some aspect of his job. Brenda Jones asks to see her form tutor and talks over the situation in the lunch break. Mrs Williams is visited at home by the district nurse, who is new to the area. David Jones, if he takes part in this exercise, has been rung up by his mother before he leaves for lectures, and goes in to see the student counsellor, worried about the family at home. During the time you are waiting to be called back for the role plays, decide between yourselves which counsellor/helper you are going to play and with whom the assistants are working. You might also discuss the factors the helpers will want to bear in mind, knowing as you do that this is a family situation and that the other members of the family are seeing helpers (although when the time comes for the counselling session, in role the helpers do not know this). There is 30 minutes for the role play, and the helper can use up to half of that for times-out. The end of the role playing will be called centrally, and if time permits there may follow a period of negotiation, when different pairs in the family can meet and talk before dinner. It might be helpful to bear this in mind since it may give the helper the opportunity to encourage the client to talk to other members of the family. During this period of negotiation, and during the following evening meal, the helpers and their assistants will once more be asked to leave the room, when the helpers need to debrief the role with the help of their assistants, discussing how it went; you can then share your experiences with other helpers and assistants. If numbers do not warrant some people being assistants, the debriefing should take place with the other helpers. You will be called back for a review of the exercise in small groups, although, if time permits, there may be one small task for you before then . . .

Brief for Bill Jones: You run your work on the principle of delegation of labour, and you expect your home life to follow the same pattern. It is your wife Mary's concern to manage the kids, while you earn the money. Girls' education is not all that important as far as you can see, but you are concerned at the thought of a 15-year-old girl being alone on the street after dark. When you go to work you have the chance of seeing your personnel manager to talk about staffing, and can bring up any concerns you have about the home situation.

Brief for Brenda Jones: You obviously want to get some extra money to enjoy yourself, buy make-up, clothes, CDs, etc. Some of your friends have newspaper rounds. But you are not really in any mood to bargain: this is a bid to be independent. You were 'talked to' by David recently, but told him that how he ran his life was his bloody funeral. If he wanted to stick around on your parents' apron-strings he could do, but you wanted some fun, like those friends who were going to leave school at the first opportunity. Play the role as you wish, but try to leave the breakfast table for school with a bang! When you go to school, you have the chance in the lunch break of talking to your form tutor about the way things are at home.

Brief for Mary Jones: You do not have a job, although in the past you

have worked for extra money for the kids, and you feel it is important that Brenda should have opportunities you never had. You and
Bill have made sacrifices to give her a good education, and Brenda
should at least repay you by making this small sacrifice herself. You
had a word with David when he was last home and asked him to
speak to Brenda about the advantages of education, but heard no
more. He supports you, although of course he is not here to say so.
When you go into town shopping you give David a ring to tell him
what has happened (although in reality he will have witnessed the
scene so you do not literally have to do this). You then see the counselling centre, and drop in on the off chance of talking to someone
about the situation.

Brief for Grandma Williams: You are not keen on modern education.
You feel it would be OK for Brenda to have her newspaper
round – you might indeed envy her youth and her chance of being
free. You also feel that you have to depend too much on Bill and
Mary. During the day your new district nurse calls, giving you the
opportunity to talk about things.

Brief for David Jones: Last time you were home you sensed trouble
brewing, because your mother asked you to speak to Brenda about
the advantages of education. When you did so, she told you in no
uncertain terms that you were still tied to your parents' apron-
strings, and that the way you run your life was your bloody funeral.
It was pointless speaking to her. Since you are away at university, you
only hear about what has happened when your mother phones
you after breakfast (in reality she does not need to do this because
you witness the scene as a member of the audience). You are
worried about the situation at home, and go to see the student
counsellor; in fact you're not sure you enjoy education that much
yourself (although you couldn't tell your mother), because it means
so much hard work, and being away from home in a strange and
expensive city where you can't afford to do anything; perhaps you
wish you were at home now, if only there weren't the rows there.

This exercise often generates quite a lot of heat in the family members, and demonstrates, partly through the evening meal, that one
meeting with a helper does not immediately alter the situation. It
also shows how much one member of the family may be carrying

for others – Brenda, for instance, carries the flag of freedom not only for herself but also for Grandma, who may also resent being in a dependent position; Brenda may be expected to do well to please her mother, who did not have similar chances; Mary may find that this act of testing-out by Brenda needs more than her own response, and the role play may throw up how passive her husband Bill has been in family matters. Finally, the complexities of even such a simple situation expose family dynamics over three generations and suggest the value of other approaches, such as systems theory, or other forms of family therapy, which look at the whole, rather than one-to-one counselling that seeks to help individuals somewhat in isolation from the family unit.[1]

Summary

The exercises in this chapter progress from relatively simple situations, in which the listening and responding skills can be integrated in one short interview, to more complex counselling interviews, or a multiple role play that works on different levels. Role-play work, together with sufficient analysis and debriefing provides a relatively safe environment in which to practise the skills, and also enables people to understand more about the dynamics of the helping relationship.

Such experiences suggest that there are other skills which might be necessary for more formal counselling. The next chapter suggests some of the more advanced skills which can be used to facilitate the counselling or a therapeutic interview, illustrating them with further exercises.

FIVE

Advanced Facilitating Skills

The exercises in this chapter introduce the reader and the student of counselling to more complex ways of understanding different communications, and to ways of responding to more difficult situations. There are many occasions when people speak freely, thoughtfully and with feeling, and find great support and help in being listened to sensitively. Nevertheless, there are also times when the person offering help is aware that there is more than meets the eye in what is being said or expressed; or when the helper feels stuck, threatened or uncertain how to proceed – a feeling which may or may not be obviously shared by the one who is accepting help. Counsellors have found that careful sensitivity to what they themselves are experiencing is nearly always also an expression of what their client is experiencing, although the client is not always aware of this. Other helpers also, using these more advanced skills, can listen both to themselves and the person they are helping at a deeper level, trying to distinguish between their own part in the situation, and the part the other is playing, as one of the exercises in this chapter illustrates.

This equally applies in conversations, where everything appears to be proceeding relatively straightforwardly. There are always occasions when a sharper perception of the issues, or a different way of handling a remark or a question, might take the conversation on into further ways of understanding experience. The ability to respond to various remarks from an alternative angle to that suggested by the basic skills alone yields the possibility of fresh and fuller insights. The various exercises in this chapter demonstrate opportunities for more productive and often more challenging ways of responding.

First and last words

The opening words or the closing words of a counselling session (often called 'door-handle' remarks) often prove to have some meaning, even if at the time they do not appear to be more than pleasantries – the sort of things people say to each other to break the ice, or as something to say as they part. This realization might prove useful in different types of interview, even if they are not formal counselling sessions. While recognizing the temptation in some forms of therapy to interpret everything and anything, the following example is an illustration of how first or last words have something important to communicate.

A middle-aged man walked into the counsellor's room with a white polythene bag in his hand. He placed it by the front leg of his chair as he sat down, and said to the counsellor: 'That's my lunch'. The counsellor was inwardly amused at the firmness with which the man spoke, and he wondered what it was about, and why his client had to tell him this. About half way through the session the man was talking about the time in his life when the person who was to become his stepfather first came for meals with his mother and the family. 'When he came we had to make a meal for three do for four, so I didn't get as much to eat as I used to. I think that's one of the reasons I resented him, even then.' The counsellor was able to point out that he had made his ownership of his lunch very plain when he came into the room; and the counsellor went on to talk about how the stepfather coming in to the family also meant having to share his mother with one more person. Incidentally, this man found some difficulty in keeping his counselling for himself – he felt obliged at first to tell his partner everything he had said when she asked what went on, another example of his childhood experience of not having his mother (like his counselling) just for himself.

Exercise 25

There follows a short set of phrases which have been used either at the beginning or the end of a counselling session. In small groups share suggestions as to what these first and last words might mean. Group members are encouraged to guess and to speculate, since the amount of information they are given is deliberately very small. It is surprising how often groups come up with ways of understanding which are close to the original situation explained below. It is good to think speculatively and intuitively, although in a real interview or counselling session it is important for the helper to exercise care in

---

openly using speculative remarks. It is usually necessary to wait, as the counsellor did in the example above, until the possible meaning of a phrase becomes clearer, and is in some way confirmed as significantly relating to what the counsellor or helper originally wondered about.

First words

1. I'm sorry I'm late. I came what I thought was a quick way, but I got hemmed in and had to turn back.
2. It's very hot – I think there's going to be a storm.
3. The bell doesn't work. I couldn't reach you.
4. It's a battle having to open all these doors on the way in here, isn't it?
5. How are you?
6. [*It is midsummer*] The leaves on that tree are beginning to turn.

Last words

7. I had a very interesting dream last night.
8. Here's a Christmas present for you. See you in the New Year.
9. I think I'll stop there and leave early if you don't mind.
10. God! What a pathetic session!
11. Is it all right if I bring my friend with me next week?
12. [*Having just fixed the dates for three further sessions*] Is it a trouble for you to see me?

As part of the feedback for this exercise it may be helpful for the group to know possible interpretations of the phrases as they were originally used in a counselling context, to check out whether or not the speculative ideas bear any relation to the original situation. The original circumstances were as follows – in each case, one possible meaning is suggested of the phrases used.

1. This client had seen two counsellors already, each time for only one session; she was looking for a quick solution, and went away each time apparently satisfied. At the end of their second session together, this third counsellor had suggested meeting regularly, and the client's words were spoken when the third session began late. She had indeed tried to take a

short cut to the building, but found herself in a cul-de-sac and had to turn back. The counsellor did not pick up the possible deeper significance of these words, and at the end of the session, when the client said that she did not need to come again, it was too late to look at her difficulties about staying in counselling, which might have been related to feeling cornered.

2. It was actually a hot day, although not a close one where a storm might be expected. This person was very upset about something that had happened outside the session, but the remark about the storm helped the counsellor to refer to, and draw out, just how angry the client was too.

3. In fact the bell to say this client had arrived was working, but this client did not press it hard enough. She was concerned in the session that followed (with a male counsellor) that she was not attractive to men. This may have been a reference therefore to not being able to push herself forward with any confidence, but of course, 'belle' also means an attractive woman.

4. There were indeed four doors to go through to get into the counselling room, but this remark also seemed to refer to the struggle this person was experiencing in opening the doors to his own feelings.

5. This is naturally a common phrase on meeting anyone, but it can have many other meanings besides being a mere pleasantry. In this instance the counsellor asked the question back and was told that things were not at all good.

6. The client who said this was due to finish counselling in the autumn after seeing the counsellor weekly for two years, and seemed both to be anticipating the season of autumn, and to be saying something about their relationship coming to a close.

7. This appeared to be an attempt to hold the counsellor's interest, either at the time in order to extend the session, or over the next week until they met again.

8. With this particular client, the gift felt as if it was a way of ensuring that she would not be forgotten over the break, but it could also have been an attempt to be kind to the counsellor when the client actually felt angry at being left without counselling over the long Christmas break. The question of

accepting such gifts is another issue, which this exercise does not examine.

9. Like the other phrases in this exercise this one could have many meanings, but in this instance the words were said by a client who was afraid of being rejected, and who always finished the counselling session himself rather than feel hurt by the counsellor saying (which she never got a chance to) that it was time to finish.

10. This might have been a reference to the way the client perceived the work by the counsellor, but in this instance it seemed more to refer to the client and how she felt she had wasted her time. In fact she had spent much of the session complaining justifiably about things which she normally felt she shouldn't complain about, so the session was only pathetic to the side of her that said to herself, 'Be quiet and don't complain'. It did not feel a pathetic session to the counsellor.

11. This client found it very difficult to talk about himself, and wanted his friend to do the talking. He was very dependent on his friend and they later became sexual partners. The question of seeing a second person as well as the original client obviously depends to some extent on the nature of the relationship between the helper and the client, and between the client and the third person.

12. The helper had a cold, which may have elicited the remark; but this client had talked in the session of not having lived anywhere for more than a few months at a time. She also easily became defensive, and denied anything that might prove to be a painful insight. So while she may have seen herself as troubling for the counsellor, who was not well, or may have thought she was in any case a trouble to the counsellor, perhaps the client was more 'troubled' about what counselling would do to her.

Awkward customers

Mini role plays can be useful in looking at particular situations which can arise in a helping interview. This exercise looks at six particularly difficult or potentially embarrassing situations which might arise in counselling, or in other helping relationships, and which present the counsellor with a different dilemma, often to do with personal or time boundaries of one sort or another. They give each person two chances to be the counsellor or other helper, the 'client' and the observer.

Exercise 26

The exercise can be set up in a variety of ways, but one particularly effective method is to use the model of a progressive barn-dance. The larger group forms into threes, in each of which the participants are lettered A, B or C. A is asked to stay in the same place for all six mini role plays, but after each session B moves round clockwise, and C anticlockwise, thus altering the composition of the threes for each different situation. Each mini role play needs a few minutes' silent preparation. Indeed the 'clients' can move into the middle of the circle to discuss with each other how they will play the role. The role play itself lasts for five minutes only – the observer keeps the time. The rest of the period allotted is needed for debriefing, and perhaps for some reflection on the hints set out at the end of the exercise. At the start of each mini role play A, B and C are given their separate instructions. (Alternatively the instruction sheets for As, Bs and Cs can be made up beforehand in the form of a small booklet, with a separate page for each session, to be turned over when moving on each time).

The hints on the handling of each of the six situations are included below in the six briefing sheets. These are set out here for all three participants in each role play, but in the exercise they need be given out only to the person whose letter is indicated before each brief. Debriefing takes place during the exercise, after each mini role play. Experience of conducting this exercise suggests that it often faces students with just how difficult some people can be. The exercise may make us more realistic about the difficulties of helping and counselling, but at the same time it may shake our confidence. Such realism is no bad thing, but it is important in debriefing to review how each person felt in the different roles they played.

Briefings for mini role play 1

Brief for A: In this session you are the observer. Help the counsellor during the briefing time. Observe during the role play, making notes if you wish; and in the debriefing share your observations, particularly on how you felt about the way the counsellor coped with the situation.

Brief for B: In this session you play the counsellor. It is the very beginning of a counselling interview, arranged by you with someone who has asked to see you; you have 45 minutes set aside for the session – although you will only play the first five minutes of it.

Brief for C: In this session you play a new client who has asked to see a counsellor. You now have cold feet, and so you use a number of ploys in the opening five minutes, such as: 'I don't know where to begin'; 'But it's such a long story I don't know whether to start with now or the past'; 'I don't know quite how to put it'; 'Do you think talking about it is going to help?'; 'I think I'm going to waste your time'; 'I think it doesn't really trouble me now as much as when I first made a time to see you'; 'Perhaps I could see you another time'; 'I do feel awful taking up your time like this' – etc. Put in any other similar phrases you wish. But if you feel the counsellor presses home the point that you are uncertain, or in some other way encourages you to make a start, you can then begin your story: you are a person who worries about making decisions – and here you can put in your own ideas, such as whether to change jobs, move house, etc.

Briefings for mini role play 2

Brief for A: In this session you play the client, a demanding person, coming to the end of the first session with a counsellor or other helper, who has already arranged to meet you next week. When she or he says it is time to finish you ask whether you could 'just go on for another half hour or so', because there are some things which you haven't yet had a chance to say. See how the counsellor responds, but have up your sleeve remarks like: 'But it can't wait till next week'; 'I might not want to say these things then'; and as a last resort, as you begin to get angry, 'But you call yourself a counsellor; I thought counsellors were meant to be caring'; 'I don't think you really care' – etc. If the counsellor is able to bring the session to a close within the five minutes allowed, either by brute force or by saying the right thing, then you go along with it; in that case get into the discussion period on the mini role play earlier.

Brief for B: In this session you are the observer. Help the counsellor during the briefing time. Observe during the role play, making notes if you wish; and in the debriefing share your observations, particularly on how you felt about the way the counsellor coped with the situation.

Brief for C: In this session you play the counsellor or another type of helper. It is the end of the first session, and you have already arranged to meet again next week. You start the mini role play with the words, 'We do have to stop there. So we'll meet again next week, same time', or something similar.

Briefings for mini role play 3

Brief for A: In this session you play the helper. You are just about to leave the office or study to catch a train to London, and you are already a little late; under no circumstances can you afford to miss the train. The phone rings . . . (Conduct this interview face to face, assuming that it is a phone call, without troubling too much about authenticity about being on the phone.)

Brief for B: In this session you play a very panicky person who rings up the helper in an awful state; you must speak to them now. If you don't do so you don't know what you will do. You woke this morning with dreadful palpitations, and you know it's nerves, because you've had them before; you've rung the doctor who says come to surgery, but you can't leave the house; and the doctor can't call until this afternoon. You must see the helper – can they call? It must be them you see – a friend has told you this helper is very good. You are due to go and see your mother for coffee, but you can't ring her in this state – her heart's not good, and it might kill her – etc., etc. Embroider as much as you like. If the helper brings the call to an end before the five minutes is up, either by not answering or by putting the phone down or by saying the right thing, then you go along with it. You will then have more time for the discussion period. (Conduct this interview face to face, assuming that it is a phone call, without troubling too much about the authenticity about being on the phone.)

Brief for C: In this session you are the observer. Assist the helper during the briefing time. Observe during the role play, making notes if you wish; and in the debriefing share your observations, particularly on how you felt about the way the helper coped with the situation.

Briefings for mini role play 4

Brief for A: In this session you are the observer. Assist the helper during the briefing time. Observe during the role play, making notes if you wish; and in the debriefing share your observations, particularly on how you felt about the way the helper coped with the situation.

Brief for B: In this session you are the helper, and the young person with you has presented you with the problem that she or he does not get on with her or his father; and that there was a blazing row this week about this young person not yet having a job, and therefore not contributing anything to the household income. The time has come to conclude this particular interview, and you start the mini role play by suggesting another meeting next week.

Brief for C: In this session you play a young person who has just spent some 45 minutes telling the helper about the blazing rows you have at home with your father; and that this last week he got at you for not yet having a job, and therefore contributing nothing to the household income. The helper suggests that you meet another time, which you are happy to agree to. But you then bring out more information – not in an effort to prolong the session, but just in a matter-of-fact way, as though you accept the situation that you have to leave now. You are not a demanding person; on the contrary – you are rather passive; but at the same time you are at the end of your tether and wonder whether there's any point going on living. The thing is that as a result of the row this week, your father told you to 'get out and not come home until you've found a job'. You said that you were going for a job interview today, but it was a lie, and you just dare not go home. But you have got nowhere else to go, nowhere to sleep, no money for anything to eat. 'I don't know what I'm going to do', you say, although not actually intending that the helper should do anything about it. A sensitive helper may feel this is one time that the session should be extended a little, and that some action needs to be taken to get you help, although you are not expecting this.

Briefings for mini role play 5

Brief for A: In this session you play the client, a person who has seen the counsellor several times. Your problem is that you find it difficult to relate to people, and that you are always on the edge of groups. Your counsellor has just come back from holiday, and this is the opening of the first session after this break. You play a person who wants to find out as much as you can about the counsellor's holiday, so you start with a phrase like, 'How are you?'; and go on to questions like, 'Did you have a good holiday?'; 'Where did you go?'; 'Was the weather good?'; 'Did you stay in a hotel?'; 'Did you go with the family?' – etc. The counsellor, if he or she responds well, will try to get the subject back to you; but you try and keep up the pressure on the counsellor – unless the counsellor is able to bring out the possibility that you have once again felt 'on the edge' because of her or his holiday.

Brief for B: In this session you are the observer. Help the counsellor during the briefing time. Observe during the role play, making notes if you wish; and in the debriefing share your observations, particularly on how you felt about the way the counsellor coped with the situation.

Brief for C: In this session you play the counsellor. You have seen your client a few times before – her or his difficulty is one of finding it hard to relate to people, and of always being on the edge of groups, etc. You have just come back from holiday, and this is the opening of the first meeting arranged after that.

Briefings for mini role play 6

Brief for A: In this session you play a counsellor. Mr Smith rang you up and asked whether you would see one of his parishioners – he gathers you have done some counselling training, and this should prove a very interesting little case for you. You meet the person referred to you for what you have made clear is an initial interview to see whether you may be able to help; and the client opens the session . . .

Brief for B: In this session you play the client who has been referred to the counsellor, whom you are meeting for the first time. Mr Smith referred you. You went to see him once, and he suggested this counsellor would be a better person than him to help you. This is a difficult part to play, but try to be someone who on one level is very earnest and apparently talks in a very knowledgeable way, but who is proverbially as mad as a hatter. You are delighted to be able to meet the counsellor – you knew they would be the right person to see because you had a vision, in which this holy man told you that you would go on a long journey, and that you would meet a person who would help you save the world. And this counsellor is clearly the person – the world has been taken over by doctors who meddle with your mind, and set themselves up as healers, but they know nothing about spiritual healing. This counsellor is the person you are clearly destined to meet and work with – the signs are all coming true. The key thing is to get in a phrase like 'I know you are the one chosen to assist me – are you prepared to help me?'

Brief for C: In this session you are the observer. Assist the counsellor during the briefing time. Observe during the role play, making notes if you wish; and in the debriefing share your observations, particularly on how you felt about the way the counsellor coped with the situation.

The following comments can be used in debriefing this exercise, either after each mini role play, or at the end of the whole exercise.[1]

1. If a new client, having made an appointment and kept it, is now reluctant to talk it is not necessarily helpful to try and coax them into conversation. It is better to grasp the nettle and look at their reluctance with them. Comments to be preferred in this situation are: 'You seem hesitant'; 'You've changed your mind since you made the appointment?'; 'But you still decided to come and see me?'; 'You're not sure now about whether you can talk to me?'; 'Perhaps it's something about me – I'm not how you expected me to be?' These and similar responses show the client that the counsellor is listening to what the client is saying, while at the same time encouraging the client to reflect on what is blocking them from talking about what it is that is troubling them.

2. At the end of a session, when the client urgently wants more and gets angry or upset, the temptation is to feel guilty and give the client a little more time, or to try and persuade the client to be reasonable about the end of the session. But what needs to be grasped here is how it might feel to the client: 'I guess that it seems very uncaring of me to say we have to stop there'; 'You obviously feel angry because it feels like I am throwing you out'; 'You will probably feel rejected that I am saying we have to stop, but we do have to'; 'I realize that you want to go on, and waiting till next week seems impossible; you may not feel like coming back to tell me then more about what it feels like to have to finish now' – etc. In fact it is often a relief to a demanding person that someone will gently but firmly set limits, and not ultimately reject them for being too greedy.

3. The first question to ask, when the phone rings and a helper answers it when they have a train to catch, is why they answered it at all! Two minutes later, having left the room, the helper would not even have known about this call. Similarly, had the helper had another person in the room already, the phonecall would have been kept very brief, if it was taken at all. It is important to take the initiative early if the phone is picked up, and to set a limit immediately: 'I'm very sorry, but I am just this minute leaving: please give me your telephone number and I will ring you back in . . .'; or 'I will get my colleague to ring you'; or 'I suggest you ring this number instead'. If that doesn't work, there may just be time to say, 'I know this is going to feel very rejecting, but I have to leave, and I am already late; please give me your number . . . I am sorry I have to put the phone down, I will ring you later.'

4. This situation is different from number 2 above. Here the helper should recognize the need for other resources which can (if they are available) at least be offered, even if they are refused. It is probably necessary to stop the interview at this point, but the helper can give a number for the young person to contact; and/or can ask the young person to contact the helper later in the day. By then the helper may have had a chance to find out about resources which can offer some management of the young person's difficulty; or may discover that the problem has been resolved in some other way by the young person. Clearly counsellors and

other helpers need information on the different welfare and
other resources that are available locally, especially emergency
services, so that this is to hand to be drawn on as necessary.

5. It is tempting in this situation (where the normally reticent
client is trying hard to be warm and friendly about the counsellor's
holiday) to allow a few pleasantries at the beginning of a session,
especially after a break; but then to find that the situation has
been turned on its head. The client's questions come thick and
fast. While it seems churlish to put some questions back, it is
important to do this early on, and to get firmer about it if the
client continues to ask questions. At the same time it is helpful to
observe how it might have felt to the client when the counsellor
was away. A series of interventions with a persistent client might
therefore run as follows: 'Yes, I had a lovely time; I wonder how
you have been?'; 'I could tell you where I've been, but I feel we are
slipping away from what has been happening to you'; 'I think you
have felt really left out with my being away'; 'I wonder if you are
asking me these questions so that you can feel you belong with
me again. Does that make any sense to you?'

6. This borderline type of personality, or to be more generous, a
religious fanatic, probably creates the hardest situation to deal
with, although the person playing the client may find the power
implicit in the role quite heady. Playing the role helps to make
clear why 'madness' can feel safer than attempts to relate to other
people in an apparently sane and sensible manner. It is possible
for some skilled therapists to work with clients who are deluded,
borderline or psychotic personalities, as Laing and Searles have
amply demonstrated.[2] It is possible for some helpers to make
sense of apparently crazy communications by steering a delicate
path between not colluding with the delusion, yet also not arguing
for a different ('normal') kind of reality or perception. It is not
helpful to say either, 'Of course you are right', or, 'No, you are
wrong'. Such communications as this person and others make,
with fantasy ideas that are out of touch with reality, often have an
internal logic, if only we could crack the code. The client in this
mini role play, for instance, may have fared badly at the hands of
some psychiatrists or may have suffered inhumane methods of
treatment. The referral from Mr Smith is a bad one, and it is

highly unlikely that a trainee counsellor would be in a position to take this client on. It is even dubious whether the client really expects to be taken on, since the client is going to call the tune. Referring this client to someone else is also tricky, partly because it becomes a second referral, partly because the very help the counsellor may want to suggest – a good psychiatric or psycho-therapeutic assessment – has virtually been ruled out by the client in her or his paranoia about medicine. There are no easy answers to the handling of this situation. What can be said is that it is important never to offer ongoing sessions before a counsellor has really assessed a situation. If there is some doubt, and this client makes the counsellor feel uneasy straight away, then no promise should be made other than: 'I can see you today, but this meeting is to see whether or not I can help you. I cannot tell you any more at this stage.' Later the truth of this situation will have to come out: 'I'm sorry to tell you, because I guess it will be very disappointing to you, that I myself do not think that I am the right person to see you. I know it may be difficult for us to find the right person who can, but I would like your help in working out who it might be best to see. Can you first tell me what makes you feel so angry about the medical profession?' In this response the counsellor sets firm limits, but also tries to tap both the dis-appointment and the adult rational side in looking for the best means of securing help.

Facing people with themselves

Counsellors and other carers may need to enable those who seek their help to face painful, uncomfortable, unpleasant or difficult aspects in themselves: painful feelings, uncomfortable thoughts or offputting behaviours. In order to do this it is necessary to develop confrontational or challenging skills.

A particular feature of counselling from a psychodynamic per-spective is the recognition both of repression (whereby unpleasant thoughts, feelings and experiences become unconscious), and of the return of the repressed – whereby that which is pushed away has a habit of returning, in a disguised form. Similarly psychodynamic counsellors and therapists recognize that it is often difficult for people to experience themselves as they really are: they do not always hear what they are saying, nor do they see what they are doing in relationships. An outside observer, such as a counsellor or a helper, is often aware of ways in which people might make life better for themselves and their relationships if they could change their behaviour or attitudes, but the counsellor also recognizes how hard it is for anyone to face certain aspects of themselves. They either hide the truth from themselves (and because this is unconscious they are unaware that they are doing it) or they try to hide the truth from the helper (normally a more conscious act).

The term often used in books on counselling skills for helping people to face themselves, is confrontation or challenging. It is not altogether a helpful expression, because it implies that a counsellor has to speak bluntly. It is important for helpers and counsellors to develop the skill of being assertive without being punitive or judgemental. It is difficult to get this balance right, and becomes even harder when it involves saying something which the other person finds it difficult to hear, and which the helper or counsellor all too often finds difficult to say.

A good way of learning how to help people face things is first of all to try to express to ourselves what we would *really* like to say to a 'difficult client'. This gives the helper the main thrust of what they would like to get across. Saying what we would really like to say identifies not only what might be called the main point of the confrontation, but also certain strong feelings about the client or parts of the client's behaviour or communication. If the feelings can be disentangled from the main point of the confrontation, it should be possible to express the main point in a way which the client finds easier to hear. After all, if the client feels attacked, however useful the helper's intervention, it is going to be even harder for the client to accept the point.

Exercise 27

Tom agrees to make a regular time to see the helper, but he always turns up late and is getting later and later each time. The time has come to help him face his lateness. What might the helper really want to say – no holds barred? 'I'm getting really angry with you playing me around.' It would be better to hold back the feeling of being 'really angry' in order to get over the main point: that it feels like Tom is 'playing around' with the time offered to him. If the helper stops to consider her or his feelings more, could the 'really angry' feeling be a clue to what Tom could also be feeling, but not expressing, except by coming late? Perhaps he is 'really angry' with the helper too, for not being effective enough, and his lateness is a silent protest. The helper can pick up this possibility and run with it in expressing the main point of the confrontation to Tom: 'Tom, I am wondering whether you are feeling annoyed with me, perhaps because you aren't sure I am taking you seriously enough. I wonder whether coming late is your way of telling me that?'

In the process described here the helper goes through a series of mental steps before speaking to Tom: this is possible in a helping or counselling interview, because not everything needs to be said at once. The process involves the following:

(a) the helper/counsellor reacts by imagining what they would really like to say to Tom;
(b) they then analyse the unexpressed sentence to identify the kernel of the actual confrontation, as well as to identify their own feelings about Tom's action in coming late;
(c) they then check whether the feelings experienced could give a clue to Tom's own feelings;
(d) they may or may not use this in composing a more accept-able way of conveying what is necessary, part of which can include a reference to a hidden feeling that might be present in Tom's behaviour.

Using this process, imagine what you would really like to say to Mabel and Barry (below), identify the kernel of the confrontation, and any feelings there may be in you, check whether this gives you a clue to Mabel's or Barry's feelings, and then compose a more acceptable way of confronting Mabel and Barry which she and he might hear without taking too great offence.

1. Mabel talks too much in a discussion group; she dominates the other members, and they cannot interrupt her, yet they are clearly getting bored with her and the group. As a group leader how would you help her see this? Go through steps (a) to (d).

2. Barry has been to see you twice about his marriage. He has so far put all the responsibility on to his depressed wife, and speaks of himself as innocent of any blame. How can you help him face

what his attitude might be doing to his wife? Go through steps (a) to (d).

Now divide into pairs, and split the next four situations between you. Let one partner get into the first character, while the other partner works out how to confront this person (using steps (a)–(d) as above). When both are ready, play out a few moments of a counselling interview, with the 'counsellor' at some point confronting or challenging the 'client', and the client reacting as they might. Stop the scene, and monitor how it felt to say what you did as counsellor, and to receive what you heard as client. Then swap roles as counsellor and client as you move on to do the same with next three characters.

3. You have come to ask for help for your friend who is pregnant or has got a girl pregnant. In fact you are talking about yourself, but you daren't admit it. (Does the counsellor help you to own the true situation?)

4. You have come to the helper because you are really fed up that you can't make friends. You are very badly depressed, you are untidy, and your clothes don't appear to have been washed for weeks. You complain that nobody wants to know you. (Does the counsellor help you to look at yourself and how your appearance contributes to this?)

5. You've been kicked out of college because you haven't done any work. Instead of expressing any real feelings about this, you make light of the whole incident, and talk about surface issues – like what a laugh college was, that you don't mind about this or that consequence, etc. (Does the counsellor help you to acknowledge deeper feelings of anxiety, guilt or hurt?)

6. You don't want to criticize your counsellor because you are afraid you will look bad in their eyes; but you feel really let down by them for not being around last week when you wanted extra help. You can't say this: instead you insist on saying what a pity it was that you couldn't see the counsellor, who is so very helpful, and that another person you contacted last week instead was useless. (Does the counsellor help you acknowledge your true feelings towards him or her about letting you down?)

The following are examples of the process of framing a confronting intervention in the various instances of what might be said to Mabel (1) and Barry (2):

1. [Mabel, who talks too much in the group]

   (a) What the facilitator might want to say to Mabel: 'Will you shut up! You are ruining this group.'
   (b) The kernel of what the facilitator might want to express: Mabel may have taken over what she thinks is the facilitator's role, imagining she is keeping the group going because the others are silent – partly, of course, due to her talking too much as well.
   (c) What the facilitator personally feels: annoyed with Mabel, but also with other group members for not interrupting Mabel more. It would be easy to get angry with Mabel when in fact the anger belongs to the group generally.
   (d) What the facilitator might therefore say aloud: 'I think that as a group we are making you, Mabel, take on all the responsibility for talking here, as though it is the one way of making the group feel it is working; but I guess we all find it frustrating in our different ways, including you, Mabel.'

2. [Barry, who cannot see that he contributes to his wife's depression]

   (a) What the helper might want to say to Barry: 'No wonder your wife is depressed; you're making me feel depressed, because I can't help you if you won't accept your part in it.'
   (b) The kernel of what the helper might want to express: something that will help Barry look at his part in the relationship.
   (c) What the helper personally feels: helplessness, which must not be conveyed, but it may tell the helper something about the way Barry or his wife are feeling.
   (d) What the helper might therefore say aloud: 'I think it must be very difficult, when your wife feels depressed, and I can imagine it makes you angry. You feel you do nothing to cause this, which might make her feel even more depressed. It must be difficult to know how to start helping both her and yourself in this situation.'

The following interventions suggest what might be said to any of the people in the next four examples, after the process of working through the different steps:

3. [The pregnant girl] I'm wondering whether it would be very difficult for you to tell me if it was really you who was pregnant?

4. [The unwashed client] I know this may sound odd, but I wonder whether there is actually a strong part of you that isn't at all sure about letting anyone get close to you as a real friend? What might you do that could perhaps put some people off?

5. [The nonchalant failed student] You seem to me to feel very light-hearted about something which you could also find rather worrying. Perhaps it is difficult to admit that this also has a more serious side to it.

6. [The timid but critical and let-down client] I think you are finding it hard to tell me that you feel disappointed in me for not being here when you really wanted me. Last week my absence made me just as useless as you say the other person was.

The process described above might also be used in connection with this exercise as a way of confronting the tutor of a course on which these exercises are being used. It is a good way to practise learning confrontational skills on a real issue, and a real person – because tutors have feelings too!

In the small groups they have been working in already, course members should decide what they would like to say to the tutor about the course, or about the teaching of it. Ideally it should be something which initially seems too negative and critical, and therefore too difficult to say directly to the tutor. The groups need to go through the same sequence as above, from (a) to (d), and finish by framing a confrontation which they can express directly in front of the class to the tutor, but without feeding back the initial comments in (a), or any other part of the process.

There is a further aspect to this exercise which makes for valuable discussion. The questions can be asked: What makes it difficult for helpers to confront and challenge? And what makes it difficult for clients to accept and think through these types of intervention? The first question leads to a host of interesting observations on the character of many of those who are in helping and caring professions.[3] There are a few who misuse the power of such a position, and treat people abusively or sadistically under the cloak of care and kindness, sometimes justifying it with the cruel slogan, 'I am only doing what is best for you'. But many other carers find it difficult to express disagreement or to handle conflict, to make valid criticisms or to challenge inappropriate behaviours or ways of thinking. This can be even more inhibited by some religious moralistic values about the need to love others and to turn the other cheek, the opposite of the other religious set of values expressed in 'Spare the rod and spoil the child' or 'An eye for an eye'. The former set of high values (which I have no wish to contradict as a prime principle) appears to prevent carers and helpers from suggesting that those they work with might reflect upon what they in turn are doing either to themselves or to others, which can be far from loving.

The second question – about what makes it difficult for people to hear such challenges and to work on them – is connected to expectations that challenge and criticism mean shame and punishment; it also relates to other anxieties which people have about examining their thoughts and behaviours more closely, and revealing their deeper feelings more obviously to themselves and others. This is all connected to a series of defences which the next section and the next exercise examine in greater detail.

Working with defences

Defences are strategies which are used, sometimes knowingly but often unknowingly, in order to avoid facing aspects of the self or of relationships with others that feel threatening.[4] These aspects of the self differ from person to person, so that what feels threatening to one (such as becoming dependent) may feel less threatening to another (such as becoming independent). Resistance is another name given to the way in which defences are seen at work in counselling itself, but it might be confusing to try to make too definite a distinction between the two terms 'defence' and 'resistance' here. The most common defences are described in technical terms in psychodynamic theory, although some of these terms have entered, or are readily understood in, everyday non-technical vocabulary: repression, projection, introjection, turning against self, denial, isolation, splitting, idealization, reaction-formation, undoing, acting-out, asceticism, regression, fixation, rationalization, and displacement (for an explanation of some of these terms, see *Still Small Voice*, Chapter 8). In practice, many of the defences overlap one another and what is important is not naming defences with great precision, but recognizing when they might be in evidence, because it is at such times that the helper or counsellor needs to approach a defensive stance with particular sensitivity.

Defensiveness can often be seen in a person's passivity and silence (someone is afraid to speak lest what they say proves painful or incurs criticism), or in the rejection of everything the helper says (because someone does not wish to face it, or is anxious about being controlled by the other person), or in talking about trivia (fear of deeper issues), or in intellectualizing (fear of feelings), or in lateness or leaving early (expressing different feelings such as Tom's in Exercise 27), or in missing appointments (anxiety or shame perhaps). Other examples, more usually seen in regular and formal counselling than in helping situations arranged on an occasional basis, include terminating a counselling contract early, acting out, flight into health, or what has been called the 'gain from illness'.

While it is not essential in helping situations, or even in counselling, to label defences accurately, it is useful to be able to identify them when they appear, so that when and if the time is right, the helper can draw attention to the defence and as importantly to the reason for it. The reasons for a defence, such as those in parentheses in the paragraph above, often involve the person's fear of expressing or experiencing particular feelings or thoughts. If helpers and counsellors can identify defences when they occur, they can then begin to look for a possible explanation for them. It is particularly important to help clients recognize that a helper or counsellor is not trying to catch them out or to make them feel awkward, but that the helper understands they may have some difficulties in facing fears, feelings and other aspects of themselves. Sometimes a helper or counsellor can explain to a client what they think may lie behind the client's responses or reactions; or they can invite a client to examine the defensiveness with them, in a combined effort to understand what is going on.

Exercise 28

This exercise, and the next exercise (29), aim to show how the various forms of defence that have been identified in psychodynamic theory can be identified as conscious or unconscious resistance in the helping or counselling relationship. By carefully identifying the presence of defences it becomes more possible to help people to acknowledge painful but feared feelings and thoughts.

From the list of possible defences, let small groups work on the following vignettes, in an attempt to identify what defences might be at work.

The main defences: repression, projection, introjection, turning against self, denial, isolation, splitting, idealization, reaction-formation, undoing, acting-out, asceticism, regression, fixation, rationalization, and displacement.

1. Alan qualifies everything you say with 'Yes, but . . .'
2. Betty tells you she is better now, after last week you had begun to touch on painful feelings of loss.
3. Charlie tells you of a row with his boss after the last session.
4. Doris tells you how helpful you are compared to your colleague.
5. Eddie says he can't be upset at his father's death because he had such a good innings.
6. Fiona goes over the time when you should have stopped, telling you how demanding her husband is.

The following are typical descriptions of the defences shown by each of these people.

1. Alan demonstrates denial and rationalization, rejecting what the helper says.

2. Betty demonstrates a flight into health or repression, in an attempt to escape further exploration of her painful feelings.

3. Charlie shows an example of displacement and acting-out. Displacement involves talking about a third party, when the feelings expressed are also felt towards the helper. Acting-out means

taking action outside the session, instead of expressing feelings within it.

4. Doris demonstrates idealization (of the helper) or splitting (one person seen as good, the other as bad, instead of accepting that the helper is both good and bad).

5. Eddie demonstrates a form of intellectualization or rationalization as a way of avoiding feelings.

6. Fiona is projecting because it is not (just) her husband who is demanding: by taking up more than her share of the time she is also being demanding, but cannot see it in herself, only in the other person.

Exercise 29

In the following examples, expanded from the situations in Exercise 27, members of small groups are invited to identify:

(a) what form the defence takes (as in Exercise 28);
(b) a possible reason for the person being defensive.

Once (a) and (b) have been agreed in each example, the group moves on to:

(c) work out an intervention that might be used to help the client see what they are doing, as well as their reason for doing it.

For example, Tom (see Exercise 27) agreed to make a regular time to see the counsellor, but he always turns up late, getting later and later each time. Let us now add that today he again turns up late, and starts by telling the counsellor that he's getting more and more frustrated at work, but that he can't tell his boss he feels this way.

(a) Tom's defences: turning up late – which is acting-out; and when he talks about his work and his boss instead of his frustration with the counsellor he is using the defence called displacement – talking at one remove about the boss when he is probably also feeling frustrated with the counsellor.

(b) Reasons for these defences: both seem to be an (un?)conscious expression of what he feels about the counsellor or the counselling, but cannot directly express – i.e. frustrated and perhaps angry.

(c) What the helper or counsellor might say: 'Tom, I wonder whether you are feeling pretty frustrated with the work we're doing here too, but you can only tell me that by coming late?'

Now the group can try this approach to the situations described in Exercise 27, examples 1 and 2, with Mabel and Barry respectively:

1. Mabel is talking too much in a discussion group; she happens now to be talking about modern education, and the way in which children are allowed to speak to their teachers and parents. When she was young the motto was that children should be seen and not heard. She dominates the other members, and they cannot interrupt her, yet they are clearly getting bored with her and the group.

2. Barry has been to see the counsellor twice about his marriage. He has so far put all the responsibility on to his depressed wife, and speaks of himself as innocent of any blame. He says that she is always complaining about him, just like his mother always did; he felt and feels that he can't do anything right.

The next step is to turn this thought process into 'mini role plays', which are slightly expanded versions of the four vignettes used in Exercise 27, examples 3 to 6, which can be acted out in a brief interchange. In groups of three or four, this can be done by each person taking on the role of helper/counsellor, client and observer(s). At the start of each vignette, the person playing the client can take some time to get into the right frame of mind, one that the client may be experiencing. The helper and observer(s) have the scripts, and so can work out how best to confront the client when the vignette gets under way. This preparation involves working through these steps:

(a) What the counsellor/helper would really like to say to the client, if being completely honest.

(b) What form the defence is or might be taking.
(c) What feelings or thoughts the client might be defending against.
(d) What reasons there might be for the defence(s).
(e) How to confront the client, including the suggestion of a possible reason for their defence(s).

The situation is then role-played and the helper/counsellor must try to help lower the client's defence, and help them to be honest, or to look at themselves, etc. The client may react according to how well the interventions are made. If the interventions are successful, or if after a short while they are clearly not getting anywhere, the observer may bring the role play to a halt, so that the interventions, as well as the feelings and thoughts in making them and hearing them, can be discussed by the people playing the counsellor and client roles respectively. Ten to 15 minutes probably needs to be allowed for each mini role play.

3. You play someone who has come to ask for help, but you frame it as help for your friend who is pregnant or who has got a girl pregnant. In fact you are talking about yourself, but you daren't admit it. You insist on confidentiality because you don't want any of the friend's family or friends finding out. The parents will be particularly angry if they know, because they have very strict moral views.

4. You play a student who has come to the helper because you are really fed up that you can't make friends. This is your first term at college and away from home, although you are glad to be away from home because your mother fussed over you all the time, wouldn't let you do anything for yourself, was very protective and always worried about the sort of people you might mix with. You are dressed very badly, you are untidy, and your clothes don't appear to have been washed for weeks. You complain that nobody wants to know you.

5. You play a student who has been kicked out of college because you haven't done any work. Instead of expressing any real feelings about this, you make light of the whole incident and talk about surface issues – like what a laugh college was, that you don't

mind about this or that consequence, etc. Among all the bravado, you slip in that at least you're different from your brother, who went to Oxford, got a first and is now doing research. You've always had to struggle to keep up with his achievements.

6. You are playing a regular client, and you don't want to criticize your counsellor because you are afraid you will look bad in their eyes; but you feel really let down by them for not being around last week when you wanted extra help. What you do say is that it was a pity you couldn't see the counsellor for an extra session last week, because you had the most awful nightmares after seeing a violent film at the cinema. You wouldn't have gone if you had known what it was going to be like; you want more peace around in the world. You contacted someone else when you couldn't see your counsellor but she was not at all helpful, and not like your counsellor.

The following are examples of how these might be tackled, including a reference to the possible defensive position adopted by the client:

1. [Mabel, who talks too much in the group] I wonder whether the members of this group are thinking that really I should be doing all the talking, and you should all be sitting listening to me like obedient children listening to teacher. I suspect that makes you, Mabel, take on what everyone thinks I should be doing; you fill the silence, while others feel fed up that I'm not saying more. So they let you get on with it, thinking they shouldn't interrupt you either.

2. [Barry, who cannot see that he contributes to his wife's depression] I think there is a danger that you are going to think that I am criticizing you, just like you feel first that your mother did and now that your wife does. But I guess that it is difficult for you to admit that there are some things you don't do right, because you're afraid that will mean that someone like me is going to jump on you and blame you.

3. [The pregnant girl, or the boy responsible] I think you may be worried that I, too, would get very angry like these parents you are talking about, so you would find it very difficult to tell me if it was really you who was pregnant.

4. [The unwashed client] I know this may sound odd, but I wonder whether there is actually a strong part of you that isn't at all
sure about letting anyone close to you, in case they try and take
you over as you feel your mother does. Or even in case they are
the wrong sort of person, like she warned you about? I wonder if
you are needing to be very independent, but actually finding it
difficult to look after yourself?

5. [The nonchalant failed student] You seem to me to feel very
light-hearted about something which you could also find rather
worrying – in case you now get compared once more with your
clever brother. Perhaps it's important for you to be completely
different.

6. [The timid but critical and let-down client] I think you are
finding it hard to tell me that you feel disappointed in me for not
being here when you really wanted me. Actually I think you are
more than disappointed: I think you might feel very angry with
me for letting you down, but you are very frightened of getting
angry, in case being angry proves as destructive as the film you
saw or the nightmare you had afterwards.

Exercise 30

The last stage of this series of exercises involves participants in looking at their own defences, and the way in which they may also resist
seeing things about themselves or their clients which are important
to the therapeutic relationship. Or there may be certain issues that,
as helpers, they are finding difficult to talk about with clients. Or they
may be finding some of the learning about listening, responding
and other skills (such as observation of time boundaries) difficult to
put into practice. This discussion – in pairs of their own choosing,
where each person feels relatively safe talking to their partner – can
lead to further reflection upon themselves in either or both of the
next two exercises.

The defensiveness of the helper is technically called 'counter-
transference', where the term is used specifically to mean a block or
blocks in the helper preventing them from engaging with some areas
of concern, or with certain feelings, such as their own or the client's
anger, or with a client's idealization of a helper, or with erotic feelings

in a helper towards a particular client. Any defence against being able to acknowledge such feelings, either in the self or in the client, can lead either to inhibited communication, or in some cases to helpers abusing their power over clients. While it is unlikely that very strong defensive counter-transference feelings will emerge in this exercise, it nevertheless provides an opportunity for group members to reflect upon the personal barriers that make listening and responding less open and therefore less useful for the client.

The exercise can be conducted as a helping interview rather than a discussion in pairs. In other words, one partner can act as the listener, helping the other to talk about their possible defences, and observing any defensiveness that is apparent in the interview. This can be done for 15 minutes, followed by five minutes' feedback to the listener from their partner on how well they helped them to look at this subject. Then they reverse roles and repeat the experience for a further 20 minutes in all.

Seeing and being seen

Some of the examples in the exercises in this chapter – such as in Exercise 25 example 6, 'the leaves on the tree are beginning to turn', or in Exercise 28 example 3, where Charlie gets angry with his boss – demonstrate what is known technically as displacement, where someone refers to, or acts in, a situation that is distinct from the helping situation, but reflects feelings that belong in the helping relationship. This link between 'outside' and 'inside' the helping relationship is seen in a number of other ways, and occurs because each relationship a person has can reflect other key relationships in which they are, or have been, involved. When we meet people who remind us of former acquaintances we tend to treat them in a particular way, until we get to know them more as themselves. This is particularly true of people who have positions of authority, which includes people who are in helping or caring professions. Bad past experiences of authority figures can lead clients to become fearful at the thought of talking to an authority figure in the present, and so they may appear anxious or defensive or belligerent, before the helper has said anything to warrant it, or when the helper says something which is intended as an innocent remark.

This common phenomenon, which is present in every relationship, whereby we transfer on to others perceptions and experiences we have had in the past (whether yesterday or 30 years ago) is tech-nically known as transference.[5] It has some resemblance to, and indeed is sometimes mistakenly called, projection, although projec-tion technically is when someone disowns a part of themselves and puts it on to another. In Exercise 28 example 6, Fiona projects her demanding nature on to her husband and criticizes him, rather than accepting it as part of herself. This can also happen to helpers – the helper is accused of being (for example) offish, critical or cold, when the person asking for help is unable to see that they are in fact this way themselves.

It is not just clients who transfer or project on to their helper. This phenomenon is prevalent in every relationship, and the helper will hear the client describing what appear to be examples of trans-ference and projection in relation to others: for example, 'I don't think my partner really appreciates me', might also be saying, 'My experience as a child, of often having my achievements ignored, has left me very sensitive to not being fully appreciated now'. Further-more helpers can transfer and project on to their clients. This has been given the technical term 'counter-transference', and has come to mean the way in which the helper uses their own feelings in order to understand something of what the client may be experiencing (as in Exercise 27, for example, where the helper is asked to identify what they are actually feeling about the client); but it should never be forgotten that helpers may have difficulty in identifying certain feelings in clients, because they have problems with those feelings themselves; or may react to some clients in ways which are reminis-cent of former key figures in the helper's life. Counsellors and helpers can project unacceptable aspects of themselves on to their clients.

Relationships are inevitably influenced by the history which each party brings to them. However much we may understand our per-sonal history, it continues to influence us, for good and ill. The best of what we offer to others comes from the good experiences we have had, while the problems that arise between us and others also stem from ways in which we, and they, have been less well treated in the past. The two exercises that follow are designed to demonstrate how different perceptions can be: they show that the same person can be seen in distinctly different ways by others, which in some cases tells us more about the person perceiving than the person perceived; and that we do not always recognize that others do not perceive us in the way in which we perceive ourselves. The significance of this in the counselling situation is illustrated by the following example.

The American psychotherapist I. D. Yalom tells of a single hour's session in which he asked Dr C, a consultant hypnotherapist, to work with his client.[6] Yalom was present for the whole session. In the course of this man's work, Yalom's client, Marie, smiled at two apparently significant moments. Yalom asked the consultant afterwards what he felt the two smiles meant. Yalom himself thought, from what he knew of the client, that they meant something different. Later he asked the client herself what the two smiles had meant, and she gave yet a third interpretation.

When she first smiled, the hypnotherapist Dr C had suggested that Marie discuss the pains in her jaw with her oral surgeon, so he could tell her what pain was functional and what pain might be of some other origin. Dr C thought that her smile meant that she had received his message.

Yalom felt she had smiled because her oral surgeon was an old college friend who had made, and still made, sexual advances to her – but he was very good at his job and essential for a lawsuit she was conducting about the accident in which her jaw was damaged. Yalom felt that the hypnotherapist's innocent suggestion evoked a smile at the complex relationship she was already in.

When Yalom later asked Marie what the smile meant, she said the smile was embarrassment – that she felt ashamed because she thought Yalom had told Dr C about the relationship with the oral surgeon. She liked Dr C, and indeed would like to have had a relationship with a man like that. So the smile said: 'Please Dr C, go on to something else. Don't ask me any more about the oral surgeon. I hope you don't know about it.'

Likewise the second smile meant something different to each of the participants. It came when Dr C suggested that Marie's smoking was harming her body as much as if she fed her dog poisoned meat. Again Dr C thought her smile meant that she understood, and he reinforced the point.

Yalom thought the smile was at a joke she and Yalom had between them. Her awful-smelling dog put men off coming to her house – and Yalom had tried to support a suggestion from her friends and family that she have the dog put to sleep. So her smile meant, rather like the first one, 'If only you knew what you were saying, Dr C'.

For Marie the smile meant something else again. She appreciated all Dr Yalom had done – and she felt he had made things work for her, partly by pressing her on areas like the dog, which was almost like him giving her direct advice. But she thought psychotherapists were not meant to give direct advice, so her smile meant 'Yes, Dr C, got it! Let's get on to something else. I don't want to be questioned like that any more. I might make Dr Yalom look bad.'

On both occasions the hypnotherapist thought the smile meant that he had got each point right; Yalom thought the smiles meant recognition of two complex situations (which he thought he had got right?); and Marie thought her smile was one of embarrassment, protective of herself or of Dr Yalom.

Yalom comments that this particular hour was 'a testament to the limits of knowing . . . a series of distorting prisms block the knowing of the other'.[7] He lists these prisms:

(a) A barrier between image and language: we always have to translate image into language to communicate.
(b) Selectivity about what we choose to disclose to each other.
(c) Translation by the receiver of the speaker's language back into images: 'the translation error is compounded by bias error'. We see people through our own reading of them.
(d) 'The vast richness and intricacy of each individual being.'

Exercise 31

This exercise and Exercise 32 introduce helpers and counsellors to the different perceptions people have of each other and of themselves, and may help to illustrate in a more personal and immediate way that everyone is both subject and object of the different phenomena of projection, transference and counter-transference. It has the potential for opening up the feelings which members of the training group have about each other, and is therefore better used where there is a reasonable level of trust, and time to work through any strong emotions or reactions that are engendered by the exercises. At the same time the exercises may help to create a deeper atmosphere of trust, and promote the ability to give and receive compliments and suggestions. The aim of both exercises is to help participants become more aware of how they see and are seen by others, to encourage the practice of clear observation, and possibly to show up barriers to self-perception and the perception of others.

Form groups of four to six people. Focus upon one person in the group at a time in each part of the exercise.

1. Starting with the one member of the small group as a focus, the other members write down the completion of this sentence: 'The first thing I notice about you is . . .' They should describe something very obvious which they see about the person in focus. This may also be the client's first impression of the helper. Everyone in the small group reads their sentence out. The person in focus may want to respond. Repeat this with each member of the group being the subject of the sentence.
2. Return to the first person. The sentence which is now to be completed is: 'You remind me of . . . who . . .' This time check the similarities or differences between the person in focus and the person mentioned in this sentence. Again, go round the group so that each person in turn is in focus. This part takes longer.
3. Return to the first person in focus, and now complete the sentence. 'You make me feel . . .' Here the feeling described should refer to the person writing the sentence. Check whether this is a feeling which the person in focus would agree he or she conveys, or whether it is saying more about the observer. Repeat round the circle as before.
4. The fourth sentence to be completed begins, 'I imagine that you might be . . .', which can be completed in any way the person wishes, and again should be checked with the person described to confirm or refine the impression.
5. Finally each person in the group says what gift (material object or abstract quality) they would like to give each other member of the group. When this is completed the group can discuss what these gifts are saying both about the donor and the recipient.
6. Discuss the exercise, the feelings it has left the group members with, and what has been more generally learned from it about the helping or counselling relationship.

Exercise 32

The exercise uses a form of self-analysis, which is then checked with

the perceptions of other members of the group. It requires a
worksheet similar to Figure 3. Check the instructions out with the
participants, and then work through the three stages of the exercise
in turn. Enough time needs to be allowed for each stage to be satis-
factorily completed, the first two by members working alone, the
third by mixing with each other. People need to be encouraged to be
really honest with each other. This exercise again works best in a
group where members have got to know and trust one another well.

Stage 1	Stage 2	Stage 3	
In this column draw up a list of ways you tend to be seen by people who do not know you well or at all, whether in your public role or as a private individual. It does not matter if some are contradictions: include them all whether or not people are right to see you in any of these ways.	Now tick any of these statements which are in your view accurate perceptions of you; put a cross by any which you think are inaccurate; and a question-mark by any where you are not sure. Finally, add in any spaces left ways you would describe your real self, if not already included in Column 1.	Mix with the rest of the group, asking people one at a time for their first impressions of you. Tick in Column 3a where you have already listed these in Columns 1 or 2, or add them as statements in Column 1. Then ask them for their considered impressions of you and tick them in Column 3b, or add in Column 2.	
		3a	3b

Figure 3 How we see ourselves and how we are seen by others

Participants should mix with everyone, meeting with people in the class whom they know and do not know, in order to get as many perceptions as they can from others. When the exercise has provided sufficient opportunity for the participants to meet and talk with several other people, move on to debriefing it in small, familiar fours where the group members can feel safe to share their reactions, particularly to anything which has caused them any difficulty or distress. While most students are careful how they phrase their comments, some of those who receive them may feel criticized or hurt. When there has been sufficient opportunity to share the different feelings aroused in this exercise, discussion can move to what may have been learned about transference, counter-transference and projection.

Summary

The deeper aspects of the helping relationship have been discussed and examined in this chapter – but the links between these more advanced skills and exercises and those in the earlier part of the book is that there is always more than the obvious in the way in which the person seeking help and the helper, perceive each other and relate to each other. These different aspects of the helping relationship have been highlighted in the practice of psychotherapy and counselling, but are generally applicable in many caring situations.

Knowledge is two-edged: it can be used sensitively to further the welfare and insight of those who seek help; but it can also be used as a blunt instrument to knock them senseless. As shown in the last two exercises in this chapter, speaking from a different perspective can help another person to know themselves better, but it can also, inappropriately understood and expressed, cause considerable hurt and distress. As with so much else in this book, practice of these skills and application of this knowledge should take place first in the training group, where errors of over-zealousness or clumsiness can be corrected. Thereafter support or supervision for carers should be seen as essential for the development of this work, as it is in all counselling and most psychotherapy practice.

An essential aspect of this learning – in this book, in the training group and in supervision – is the helper's ability to recognize where they must draw the limits of their knowledge, experience and skill, and when they should therefore pass the person seeking help on to an agency, a specialist or an alternative resource where they can be given the right attention. Previous chapters have illustrated just how much more the carer, helper and counsellor can appreciate in what they are told and in what they hear and perceive, and how they can use this increased understanding for the good of the client. It is equally important to recognize how much we do not know, and that in some cases there is much that we cannot undertake. Deciding when to use these skills, and when to refer to others who have particular skills and knowledge, is the final and vital lesson of this book.

SIX

Where Next?

There is a mystique which is all too prevalent in our society, that it is only the expert who matters. Lengthy training, expensive education and statutory regulation, however important they are for the protection of the public, all tend to produce one set of people (the 'trained') who have a vested interest in promoting their unique expertise; and another set of people (the consumers, the customers or the 'users' in current jargon), who by virtue of their position fear to intrude upon the sacred ground of the professional. Whereas more people than ever before are willing to undertake tasks which previously were the domain of the craftsmen – and so find the confidence often gained from do-it-yourself – there are still too many areas where the professions appear to guard their secrets jealously. While I have no wish to underestimate the impact made by the development of professional skills (particularly in the helping field), we have as a society effectively deskilled the ordinary man or woman in those tasks which are part of our common life. Professional helpers could spread their effectiveness much further if they were able to concentrate on making their skills more readily available, leaving themselves more space to work with those whose particular difficulties appear to have gone beyond the range of caring resources that are, or could be, present naturally in the community.

Such a cautionary note is necessary lest the reader, having got this far, wonders whether he or she dare apply these skills in the context of the local community, the church, a school, a hospital, a company, etc. It is often thought that the professional must have an extra dimension which makes these basic skills effective. To deny this would be folly, since there are no doubt occasions when experience and expertise combine to help find a way through specialized problems which the lay person (in relation to a particular profession) would find impossible. There are occasions too when even the best do-it-yourself handyman or woman has to call in the expert, or when tools are needed which are not part of the normal domestic tool kit. Yet there are many more occasions when ordinary skills and tools are sufficient; what is frequently missing is the confidence to apply them.

The skills described in this book can be practised and developed through experience – indeed, the very process of opening up communication between people often provides effective help. Research has demonstrated just how effective the trainee counsellor can be, when they are first beginning to apply their skills – sometimes more so than the recently qualified counsellor. Enabling people to express their fears and their feelings, encouraging them to test the reality of their assumptions, providing them with the opportunity to put the different facets of a problem 'on the table', rather than keeping them tangled up within – all these aspects of the helping relationship can help people towards workable solutions.

Giving anyone the opportunity to speak freely, and to be heard seriously, has what is called a cathartic effect. The word is borrowed from medicine, and means purging the body of those substances which have built up within and need freeing. Careful and patient listening, and the type of responses which encourage further expression of feelings, in themselves help to release many of the blocked-up feelings of which a person is aware, but which cannot easily be shared with another. Every good listener can help another person to do this. Although a more thorough training might be needed to help people express those more hidden areas of their experience which may have been repressed in the unconscious memory, patient listening nevertheless provides a safe environment in which people can speak. It helps people recover feelings and painful memories that have been buried over time, because they have not believed they will be properly heard. The catharsis of what is known and conscious is in many cases sufficient to ease a burden, and to clear some of the impediments to resolving a problem. As long as the listener does not dig around or thoughtlessly implant ideas, people can use the opportunity provided by good listening to uncover as much as they need, and are capable at that time of acknowledging.

Good listening and accurate responding also offer people the possibility of clarifying what is fact and what is feeling, which can make for better decision-making. When a person begins to talk about their fears and feelings, both the helper and the person seeking help can begin to discriminate between what is real and what is imagined. How often the helper hears phrases such as, 'I know this sounds foolish, but I think . . .' – and yet as soon as the fear has been expressed such thoughts assume a more healthy and realistic dimension. Expressing anxieties helps a person do their own reality testing, and may enable the helper to challenge gently some of the more damaging or inhibiting assumptions that are being made. A professional resource may be needed when people's assumptions are restricting them from developing, or when fantasies rule over reality. But there are many instances where good listening, and the opportunity provided for people to hear themselves, releases them to make a more rational assessment of the issues which affect them.

Many people doubt their ability to help through listening and accurate responding because they do not give the interview a chance; neither are they used to following up requests for help by suggesting a second meeting. If they did they would find, as counsellors could testify, that people coming a second time have often reflected upon the first meeting, and having expressed themselves then, have already begun to feel a shift in the way they feel or the way in which they view their difficulties. Longer-term issues, and those states of mind that do not shift so readily, need more skilled help than the type of listening and responding skills outlined in this book. Trained counsellors and therapists are more used to working with fixed patterns and with the more intransigent examples of the defences that were sketched out in Chapter 5.

There is yet a further way in which careful listening and sensitive responding often helps. Many helpers have considerable knowledge and expertise – for example, of medical problems, social security benefits, theological questions or academic subjects. In order to use this knowledge to best effect, good listening provides them with more detailed information, which can clarify the type of action and information which might best be recommended. Some situations might include the need for advice or guidance – though the guidelines in this book caution against giving this too early. It is important to give time to listening, to helping the person expand on the issues, to enable them to express their feelings and perhaps to help them put those feelings into perspective. All this should come before giving information. And when advice and guidance is given, time needs to be allowed for the information to be thought about, clarified, questioned where it is not clear or relevant, and then absorbed.

Having listened thoroughly to someone before attempting to give advice or guidance, the helper is in a better position to know whether more specialized information is called for; to know whether a referral might be necessary; to clarify whether they may need to find out more before meeting the person a second time. It is important not to send someone to another source of help, only for them to be referred on yet again, because the first helper did not spend long enough weighing up the different dimensions of an issue. Clarifying the nature of a problem ensures that the best available professional advice can then be sought.

Moreover through the helper listening and responding sensitively, the person seeking help can grow in their own self-esteem. The helper's good listening often enhances the self-esteem of people who need help or advice. They are treated with respect, they are given time and attention, and what they say is accepted without argument or criticism. All this has the potential for engendering feelings of worth and value, which are in themselves confidence-boosting. The helper's confidence in containing many of life's situations, as they are described by those who tell their stories, conveys itself to those who ask for someone to listen.

When more specialist resources may be necessary

This book has shown that in many walks of life, in most service and caring occupations and in helping agencies, there are opportunities for greater active listening and appropriate responding than exists at present. Responsible listening, far from creating problems (as some sceptics suggest – as if counselling and other similar services have created difficulties rather than provided an opening for them to be shared, often for the first time), can frequently prevent a problem from getting out of proportion. It would, however, be irresponsible to imagine that there are no limits to what can be achieved through the relatively simple guidelines that have been communicated in this book. In practice most helpers are aware of their limitations, and if anything they tend to err on the side of caution. Some people are even afraid to listen carefully, allowing the other person a chance to speak fully, in case what emerges will be beyond them. Conversely there are a few helpers who either have omnipotent fantasies about what they can achieve, or who misuse their position by exerting dominating power over others. In considering the need for supervision and support (as I do briefly below), it is clear that the timid could benefit from realizing how much more they could facilitate, while the headstrong need to be watched and reined in.

If most listeners are aware of their limitations, it is probably also true that most of those people who seek help are only prepared to go so far: they are more likely to terminate the sessions before touching material that is too difficult to handle than they are to 'spill out' over the helper and the agency. The defences referred to in Chapter 5 act as natural means of preventing too much from emerging too soon. Those who come to talk are probably more afraid than their listeners of what they will open up if they talk too freely. The story of Pandora's box illustrates people's fear that, if they lift the lid, all manner of uncontrollable feelings will fly around. The experience of those who listen as trained counsellors and therapists suggests that this danger can be overstated, and that the fear of lifting the lid is often worse than what is thereby actually revealed. In many instances, the release of pent-up feelings and the expression of horrifying thoughts and wishes is a freeing experience, and leads to no damage either to the self or to others. Catharsis is usually beneficial.

However, there are occasions when the good listener recognizes the need to close the lid, or even to refer a person on to more specialized or experienced help. Someone who, in the two minutes before the scheduled end of an interview, looks very upset and wonders whether she should begin to tell the helper about a dreadful incident in the past, needs to be contained so that nothing too hard occupies the remaining time: 'I think that you might want to tell me this when there is more time rather than upset yourself now. Do you think you can try to tuck it away for the moment, and see whether you want to tell me next time we meet?' In other instances it may be necessary to be firm and open about what the helper cannot achieve: 'You are telling me that you are afraid that you may burst out angrily and do some harm, as you know you have done in the past. I wonder whether we can look together at whether particular help would benefit you, because what you are describing can be helped more by those with special training. I think that might make it feel safer for you'.

Over and above the personal inner response of the helper – which may indicate that they could be getting out of their depth – there are certain guidelines which might assist the helper in discriminating between those who could be helped by talking things over, and those who might need more skilled help. The lists below summarize characteristics that may distinguish between those who can use the opportunity of good listening and sensitive responding over a short series of meetings arranged together, and those who probably need more intensive or longer-term counselling or psychotherapy – or even medical or psychiatric assessment and/or intervention. The list aims to identify those who can benefit from the help of someone using facilitating skills described in the first four chapters of this book:

Probably suitable for a good listener	*Probably unsuitable*
A short-term problem, one which has arisen recently, with some possible reasons for its onset. There may be long-term problems as well, but the person seeking help wants to talk about the short-term issues.	Long-term emotional problems which go back many years, or problems which appear to have no obvious cause. Some long-term problems – such as physical illness for which there is little hope of cure – may nevertheless suggest the need for the sufferer to talk about their feelings, as long as the helper is able to offer the time.
The person who can put experiences and feelings into words and who shows obvious feelings.	The silent person who cannot be drawn into speaking about themselves, or who appears to have great difficulty experiencing their feelings.
Someone who accepts their own part in a problem, who feels the issues to be partly in them and not just external to them, who can recognize how other people might feel, and their own effect on others.	Someone who blames others or external circumstances alone, who externalizes problems, who lacks awareness of others and of their effect on others. Someone so self-centred that the helper feels no sense of personal contact – just words.
A person who wants to change, even if it is difficult to see how to change.	A person who does not want to change, or even sees nothing wrong with their own attitudes; who minimizes the effects of their problem (e.g. penitent heavy

drinkers who are not going to change).

Someone who does not expect the listener to solve the problem, but accepts that the listener may be able to help by listening – especially when this is explained to them.

Someone who expects magical solutions or change to come about through outside means – a prescription, simplistic advice, changing the circumstances, or through religion or some other belief system supplying simplistic answers.

A person who is independent enough to be coping on the whole with life, even if things may be far from ideal; who can get through, from week to week, but is not so independent as to distrust the helper.

The aggressively independent person or the very dependent/demanding person, especially those who keep asking for extra help or more time – outside arranged interviews – or who seek help from many people at once.

A person who finds it difficult to accept the limits set by the helper on what they can offer.

A person who is able to relate to at least one other person, and to relate to the working environment; who has a type of staying power which indicates that there is probably also some commitment to the helper and the helping process.

Someone who shows little or no ability to relate to anyone; who has a poor work-record, who tends to run away from difficulties rather than face them.

The impulsive person, who acts out feelings rather than trying to express feelings in words to the helper.

Someone showing bizarre thoughts or behaviour, especially if they are unaware of being bizarre; or someone who is very frightened and out of control.

If someone has physical symptoms which are linked in some way to the problem, the helper needs to clarify that physical causes have been investigated.

Such lists can only be used as general guides, and there are times when the line is unclear between what can be offered and the need for referral. Nevertheless, a helper who wishes to develop the helping relationship through listening and perhaps through several meetings will be looking for a good number of the qualities described in the left-hand column, and will feel cautious about any single indication in the right-hand column. Making such decisions is considerably helped where support and supervision of helpers or listeners is offered as part of the work (but often it is not). Other factors certainly come into play, such as the amount of time that the helper has to give and the pressures of other people needing care, as well as the level of skills which the helper has developed. Counsellors and therapists always arrange regular times when working with clients, but many other helpers do not have such clear control over their working day, and may therefore have less opportunity to meet people weekly. In some places, such as some schools or some offices, it is very difficult to find sufficient privacy to engage in listening at any depth. The other constraint belongs within the helper: it depends upon the individual just how much they are able to take on board. And inevitably there are some aspects of care which come more naturally to certain helpers than to others. Some feel more confident than others at dealing with the different areas of concern that come their way.

Exercise 33

Consider the following vignettes, preferably in discussion with others. There are clues in each example which may indicate whether any of these people is suitable for the skilled listener or whether any of them need more specialized help, such as a trained counsellor or therapist, or a psychiatrist, clinical psychologist or member of a mental health team.

1. Gareth cannot concentrate upon his clerical job. He is very keen to get some help because he wants promotion. Random thoughts keep interfering (nothing in particular). There is no obvious trigger for such feelings. His thoughts are so distracting that he has several times walked across the road without looking, and has narrowly missed being knocked over.

2. Raj has been sent to you because he wants to leave his job after being with your organization for three weeks. He tells you he has previously left many places after a few weeks (a college of further education twice, a university course, evening classes) and he also gives up activities (guitar, running, pottery) once they get difficult. He is interested in getting another job and wants to be sure you won't include what he has told you in a reference.

3. Meg keeps bursting into tears at her desk. She lost her mother a month ago, and wishes she could get over it because she is getting married in six months' time.

4. Janet lost her husband three years ago, and comes to see you because she feels lifeless. She was and is devoted to him, and still has all his clothes in her house.

5. Yacoub has come to complain about his boss who keeps getting at him, and will not promote him to the sort of work Yacoub feels he is capable of. He tells you how helpful you are to him – he can tell by the white aura that surrounds your head.

6. Vivienne was verbally attacked by a man yesterday going home from work. She is normally a lively person, but she sits in front of you (a man) saying nothing, only sullenly answering your attempts to make conversation.

7. Linda is a very lively person who talks nineteen-to-the dozen to you about her difficulties making close relationships. She was abandoned by her mother when she was less than a year old, and was brought up in a mixture of foster homes and hostels.

8. Derek has decided he drinks too much. He is determined to curb his social drinking and to give up solitary drinking. He has tried before, but he never told anyone then – this time he feels that if he could just have someone to come and report progress to each week, it would be sufficient. The drinking has not interfered with his work.

Suggested answers to these situations are printed as part of Exercise 34 below.

Referral

If a person requires more specialized help, they may be more willing to take notice of the suggestion of going elsewhere from someone who has already listened well to them. Those who use facilitating skills may wish to consult a supervisor or support group, or to find out what resources are available. In this case it is better to arrange a second meeting, without any commitment to meet for longer than one more session. When it is clear that there may be other resources which could be useful and appropriate, it is preferable to provide names, addresses and perhaps telephone numbers, so that the person can make their own approach for help. This is much better than actually doing it for them, not least because it tests out the seriousness of their request for help; and also because it gives the person a sense of control over their own life. This is often reassuring when other aspects appear to be out of control. On occasion the helper may need to check out a potential resource personally, to see whether it can offer the help needed, whether there are spaces, and whether there is a waiting list. Giving out addresses just to get rid of difficult clients passes the buck, and leads the client to further disillusionment with the caring profession as they are passed from pillar to post.

It is as well to acknowledge to the person that referral will probably mean their telling the circumstances all over again, and to empathize that this may be trying – while assuring them that having someone with particular expertise to help will be better in the long run. It is rare that helpers are asked to write referral letters, or to pass on information to the new resource (although doctors and teachers may be more used to this as a matter of course), and even where such letters of referral are necessary, it is better to avoid imparting too much information. Apart from issues around confidentiality, many of those who have specialist expertise prefer to make their own assessment of a situation, and do not particularly want to be encumbered with personal opinions or surplus details.

Usually there should be no attempt to follow up a referral. It is best to leave the person to make their own appointment and to work through whatever happens then, without checking up on them either directly or indirectly. But there are clearly some situations in which it is desirable to check that the referral has been taken up or has proved useful, and some situations in which it would be unnatural not to ask how it went or how it is going. Then the important point is not to get caught up in the issues of what is being discussed and done in the new helping situation.

It is an indispensable part of any helping work for the helper to be acquainted with the different resources in the area. Those who work in agencies should check that their agency has a list of resources in cases where it cannot itself offer help. Information can sometimes be obtained from libraries, from the Yellow Pages or the Thomson's Directory, from Citizens Advice Bureaux, or from local Councils for Voluntary Service. Some local newspapers also produce a citizen's guide. It is useful to contact likely agencies or individuals, even at times when they are not actually needed, to find out their addresses, the way they handle referrals, any costs that may be incurred, and their client groups. Such information (especially where there is personal knowledge of the people or places) makes a referral more straightforward, and gives helpers more confidence in suggesting it.

Exercise 34

In this exercise the situations described and discussed in Exercise 33 are used as mini role plays to see whether a referral can be suggested and effected without too great a feeling of threat or rejection in the client. Working in pairs or threes (that is, with or without an observer), participants take it in turns to play the role of client, helper and observer, with a view to achieving the desired outcome suggested in brackets, which incidentally reveals the 'answers' to Exercise 33. The mini role play need not last too long, and in any case should be brought to a halt by the observer or the person conducting the exercise after five minutes, allowing participants a further five minutes to discuss how the helper conveyed the appropriate message, and how the person playing the role of the client felt during the process.

1. Gareth cannot concentrate upon his clerical job. He is very keen to get some help, because he wants promotion. Random thoughts keep interfering (nothing in particular). There is no obvious trigger for such feelings. His thoughts are so

distracting that he has several times walked across the road without looking, and has narrowly missed being knocked over. [Gareth is not a suitable person to be seen by helpers using counselling skills. Despite Gareth's wish for counselling, the mention of random thoughts that are so distracting that he nearly gets killed suggests a level of difficulty which merits skilled counselling or psychotherapy assessment, or if the level of distraction is severe, perhaps even medical or psychiatric help to check out for physical causes.]

2. Raj has been sent to you because he wants to leave his job, after being with your organization for three weeks. He tells you he has left many places before after a few weeks (a college of further education twice, a university course, evening classes) and he also gives up activities (guitar, running, pottery) once they get difficult. He is interested in getting another job, and wants to be sure you won't include what he has told you in a reference. [In the first place Raj has been sent; did he want to come and talk? He has a history of not staying the course, in a whole variety of ways. He appears concerned about trusting you, and unless you are in a position to write a reference, his concern about this seems strange. In this case it is unclear whether Raj really wants help, and why he wants it – careers advice, perhaps?]

3. Meg keeps bursting into tears at her desk. She lost her mother a month ago, and wishes she could get over it because she is getting married in six months' time. [Despite the intense feelings, and the somewhat uncontrolled nature of her presentation, natural grief appears to be the main aspect here, and Meg might usefully be offered ongoing times to help her talk through some of her grief, especially with the proximity of her marriage. Might the helper offer her time-limited counselling, or refer her for brief counselling elsewhere?]

4. Janet lost her husband three years ago, and comes to see you because she feels lifeless. She was and is devoted to him, and still has all his clothes in her house. [This situation is different from Meg above. Here there seems to be ongoing depression, long after it might have been expected that Janet would show

signs of adjusting to her loss. Hanging on to her husband's clothes may or may not indicate a disturbance in the grieving process. Cruse, or some other agency especially concerned with bereavement, might seem appropriate – certainly longer-term counselling or therapy.]

5. Yacoub has come to complain about his boss who keeps getting at him, and will not promote him to the sort of work Yacoub feels he is capable of. He tells you how helpful you are to him – he can tell by the white aura that surrounds your head. [This is a hard one because in Yacoub's culture the aura may be a natural expression of the way in which people can be perceived; but on the other hand there is some suggestion here of splitting between the bad boss and the good helper, which merits caution. There appear to be persecutory factors. Is Yacoub on the edge of a paranoid episode? In fact, the original situation from which this vignette is adapted ended with this person being admitted to a psychiatric unit under section, because he had flipped and trashed his bed-sit. It would be useful to see what cultural determinants are recognized here by members of the group.]

6. Vivienne was verbally attacked by a man yesterday going home from work. She is normally a lively person, but she sits in front of you (a man) saying nothing, only sullenly answering your attempts to make conversation. [Vivienne is probably still in a state of shock, and this may not be the best time to do more than offer empathic concern. It is difficult to know why a verbal attack should have provoked such shock – a physical attack would be more likely to give rise to this reaction. But bear in mind that it may not help that the helper is a man. Perhaps the offer of assistance from a female colleague might be an initial step, to see if this helps Vivienne to talk more or to relax a little. This might be an instance for a further meeting in a few days' time to see how she is, and to determine whether something else has been triggered and what help she would like. She certainly needs to be given opportunities to take control of offers of help for herself.]

7. Linda is a very lively person who talks nineteen-to-the dozen

to you about her difficulties making close relationships. She
was abandoned by her mother when she was less than a year
old, and was brought up in a mixture of foster homes and
hostels. [It appears as if Linda is able to create a good working relationship straight away – although does it? She may
talk so much that it is difficult for the helper to respond. And
her difficulty, as she describes it, has a very long history. This
sounds like a good referral for an experienced counsellor or
psychotherapist, although Linda may experience such a suggestion as yet another abandonment.]

8. Derek has decided he drinks too much. He is determined to
curb his social drinking and to give up solitary drinking. He
has tried before, but he never told anyone then – this time he
feels that if he could just have someone to come and report
progress to each week, it would be sufficient. The drinking
has not interfered with his work. [There may appear to be
some circumstances here which merit referral to an Alcohol
Advice Centre; but there are also factors which make Derek a
suitable person for the helper to meet again. His drinking has
not interfered with his work, so there is a sense that he can
control when he drinks and how much he drinks. He wants
to make this change himself, not because someone is putting
pressure on him. He actually asks for someone to support
him by being there to report progress to. And in the original
case from which this is adapted this is what happened. The
person used the opportunity to report progress every week
for a relatively short time, and this acted as a spur for him to
continue to control the drinking successfully.]

Support and supervision

Listeners can gain much from regular membership of a support,
supervision or consultation group, where they and other helpers can
speak about their work with each other. Such groups encourage learning from experience, as well as from the interaction of the group
members. Resources such as these are an important and necessary
part of any regular work that involves listening, because constant
attention to others inevitably means containing our own needs.
Opportunities to share with peers provide the chance to speak more

freely, and to have others listen in turn. Simple though the guide-lines in this book may have sometimes appeared on the printed page, in practice their application is not always straightforward. Caring, helping and pastoral work regularly throw up new and testing situations, calling for fresh responses. There is always much to learn, given the uniqueness of every person who asks for help.

All those who listen to others need to go on developing their counselling skills. Supervision is very important in counselling and in psychotherapy, as a means not just of learning more, but of taking a step back from intensive work to find support for oneself, as well as discovering fresh insights into the work with clients. Its value elsewhere in other caring professions has also been recog-nized.[1] I hope to write more on the use of group supervision in a further volume in this series, but here introduce two simple methods of using peer groups to enable a small group of helpers to learn from each other.

Exercise 35

Having engaged in role-play work using fictitious situations throughout this book, it is a small step to use the same method in a supervision group, either with the helper taking the role of their own client in order to experience how it seems from the client's position, or by asking someone else to take the role. In this way it is possible to work through some key issues in the peer-group setting, perhaps using time-out as in other role-play work. The others present can comment as observers upon the helper's facilitating skills as well as on the client's experience.

Alternatively a peer group can be used as a place to describe a piece of helping work or counselling with a particular client. Those present can share any thoughts they have, or particular feelings which the client or the helping relationship evokes in them. It is important not to be afraid to put ideas forward, even if some are hunches or guesswork. Even if members of the group are inexperienced in counselling, they have much they can give each other.

Many opportunities now exist for further training for counsellors and therapists, of various orientations, and for working in different settings. The British Association for Counselling publishes a direc-tory of courses,[2] and local universities or colleges of further education may be able to provide information about courses in their own institutions. In-service training may be available for members of certain caring and teaching professions, as well as to those who work in management. Since there are many different approaches on offer, it is wise to make careful enquiries about further training, and to avoid courses which promise a complete training in only a short period of time. Counselling training takes a number of years, and psychotherapy training even longer. Many Anglican dioceses have an Adviser or Director of Pastoral Care and Counselling from whom reliable information is available, and other churches often have similar posts. Such training does not always denote the wish to enter the counselling profession. Counselling techniques can be adapted, with care, to a variety of work settings, and greater knowledge of the value and limitation of counselling is also useful for making referrals. There are also opportunities for working as an unpaid counsellor in a number of very professionally managed counselling agencies and services.

Learning to listen, and how best to respond, needs to be taken step by step, just as the patient listener does not rush the person who is speaking, but takes them at their own pace through what they have to say. Fortunately the ordinary human skills of listening and knowing how best to respond have not been lost in the cacophony of noise, and the rush of technological life. Electronic wizardry with its instant information ought to be able to release us to spend the time saved on the tasks of caring which machines and microchips cannot undertake: they may receive, but they do not hear, and their responses are preprogrammed. There should be a time to keep silent, and a time to reflect, and a time to speak.

Appendix

———

The following two course outlines draw on material in this book, and may be useful models of a training course. The first uses exercises solely from this book. The second suggests additional material from other sources. Part 3 provides an ice-breaking exercise which is used for the first course, and is the only exercise not included in the guidelines because its purpose is different.

1. A course in counselling skills

The following course is used in the University of Leicester counselling programme. It consists of ten two-hour sessions.

Session 1: Introductions; counselling and counselling skills

The first part of the session is for an ice-breaker exercise, such as the Dry Cocktail Party, reproduced as Part 3 below. Informal groups for discussion of exercise; feedback from groups. Second part of session: definition(s) of counselling, and the difference between counselling and use of counselling skills. Students are recommended to write a diary of their experience on the course.

Note: It is better for students not to refer to this book, if they possess it, until given the go-ahead to do so after certain sessions, listed below.

Session 2: Identifying counselling skills; listening skills

Audiotape of one of the pairs of 'Good and Bad Interviews' – see also *Swift to Hear* Exercise 1. Students listen to the interviews and then identify good and bad skills in groups. Handout on listening and responding guidelines. Introduction of listening skills. The tape-recorder – Exercises 2a and 2b (30 minutes). Listening to the

163

bass line, Exercise 3 (15 minutes); or divide class into pairs where one listens to the other, on how they feel about being on this course; the listener to listen out for bass-line feelings not directly expressed, and to draw these out when partner has finished speaking; change the pairings round so that partners who were speaking are now listening to a different person who was previously listening (20 minutes).

Chapter 1 of this book might be read after this session.

Session 3: Feelings and non-verbal communication

Small informal groups to list emotions, feelings people have – suggest they agree on a list of ten basic emotions – Exercise 4 (15 minutes). Exercise 5 (15 minutes). Feedback on Exercises 4 and 5. Video of 'silent movies' – Exercise 6 (35 minutes) – the first section of the video of that name. Followed by work in pairs, or threes with an observer, on listening to each other talking about the feelings each finds most difficult to hear or deal with when listening. The importance of trying to be accurate in identifying feelings: might use here Exercise 7 or 10.

Session 4: Empathy; the counselling setting

The first stage of empathy, listening to oneself – Exercise 8 (30 minutes); giving empathic responses: Exercise 11 (40 minutes); seating and silence (Exercise 9: 15 minutes). Other aspects of the setting – length and frequency of sessions, interruptions, etc. Questions on listening guidelines.

Chapter 2 of this book might be read after this session.

Session 5: Four-square: trying out some skills

Using some simple situations in fours – Exercise 20 (80 minutes). Feedback in the whole group. Any questions to this point on the course.

Session 6: Questions

Recap of Guidelines for Responding, initially referred to in Session 2. Questions: Exercises 12 and 13 (10 minutes and 20 minutes). Exercise 13 looks at open and closed questions. Exercise 14 on alternatives to questions (20 minutes) and Exercise 15 on handling client's questions (30 minutes).

Session 7: Paraphrasing and summarizing

Minimal responses. Paraphrasing: Exercise 16 (30 minutes). Linking: Exercise 19 (30 minutes). Response training: second section (first part) of *Silent Movies and Response Training* video (60 minutes).

Session 8: Loaded remarks

Introductory talk to the topic of loaded remarks, and questions (20 minutes); Exercise 17 (40 minutes). The video *The Clumsy Counsellor* (60 minutes). (See Note 1, Chapter 3.)

Students are asked, in the week before the next session, to think of an example, if possible a long time ago, they can talk about of helping someone (not necessarily by counselling, but in which they made some sort of relationship) when they were still young and inexperienced.

Chapter 3 of this book might be read after this session.

Session 9: Putting the guidelines together

Recap of the Listening and Responding Guidelines. Introduction of the interventions record form (Figure 1). Exercise 21: an early helping experience. For this exercise, use the interventions record form. Lessons from the exercise.

Session 10: Listening and responding practice; review of the course

Miniature role plays – see Exercise 22 for suggested scripts and method. For this exercise, again use the interventions record form. Alternatively, a 'live' situation can be used for practice in pairs or threes (with an observer), where each person has the chance to be the 'counsellor' to another student, reflecting on how they have experienced the course and what they look forward to going on to next; or, if stopping there, how they feel about ending the course. By changing the pairs or threes after each period of listening and feedback (asking students to move one pair clockwise round the room; or one to move clockwise and one anticlockwise if in threes) this provides more variety. Informal groups review the exercise, and the whole course. Questions outstanding. Recommended reading and other courses for those who wish to take their training further.

Chapter 4 of this book might be read after this session. Those going on to further courses in counselling may wish to reserve reading Chapters 5 and 6 until later in their training.

2. A course for home or pastoral visitors

'I didn't seem to say very much . . .'

The course consists of six two-hour sessions.

This course is designed to enable those who visit people in their homes, or who find people share personal problems with them at work or in their neighbourhood, to have more confidence as they meet people in such situations. It is not designed to train counsellors, although some of what is included are basic counselling skills. It attempts to help people to meet others not as social workers, counsellors, etc., but as good listeners, good neighbours, good colleagues and friends.

The emphasis in this course is on listening skills. Listening is therapeutic for the person who is being heard and therefore can be seen as preventative and healing in itself. The usefulness of people learning to listen and respond better cannot be overstressed, especially if they become involved in home visiting.

Session 1: Introduction

Introduction to the course, and to each other (ice-breaker exercise). Expectations and apprehensions. Listening with both ears (Exercise 2a). Creating a learning record. 'Homework' outline.

Session 2: Listening and responding, or 'What do we think we're doing?'

Clarifying attitudes. Listening to feelings. Listing feelings (Scripture Union Training Unit *Christian Caring* course). Skills to learn and practise in all relationships, and the basis of all counselling. The video *Take My Advice* (produced by the Training Department of the National Association of Citizens' Advice Bureaux, 115/123 Pentonville Road, London, N1 9LZ). Guidelines to good listening and various ways of responding to what we hear and observe (Chapter 1). 'Homework' outline.

Session 3: Knocking at the door, or 'What's going on in there?'

Different kinds of responding. Developing awareness of situations visitors may meet as the 'door opens', both in themselves and the person they are visiting. Inappropriate responses (Exercise 17), open and closed questions (Exercise 13), and other exercises specific to this course on empathy, etc., from the Scripture Union Training Unit *Christian Caring* course. 'Homework' outline.

Session 4: Loss and change

A look at the changes which are a normal part of life, and the experience of loss, with particular reference to bereavement. Types of loss, and patterns of response to loss. The grieving process. 'Homework' outline.

Session 5: Pandora's Box

Looking further at experiences of loss, and situations which are particularly difficult in visiting. Putting the skills into practice. Role-play work. 'Homework' outline.

Session 6: Moving on

The role and nature of lay pastoral care. Getting help from others, both for the person visited and perhaps also the visitor – referral, support and supervision. Problem-solving (Scripture Union Training Unit *Christian Caring* course). Assessing the course. Farewells.

This course was designed and written by Margaret Worthington, Ron File and Sue Cumming, and is on sale in the form of a tutor's handbook, a set of master copies for making acetate sheets for overhead projectors, and as sets of student handouts for the course. Enquiries about these and other teaching materials can be made to the Department of Adult Education, Vaughan College, St Nicholas Circle, Leicester LE1 4LB, UK.

3. An Ice-breaker exercise

This large group exercise can be used at the start of a course on using listening and responding skills, as a way of introducing the group members to each other, as well as highlighting by its conclusion some of the problems of listening and remembering.

The exercise needs at least eight people, preferably more, in multiples of four. Odd numbers will mean some people acting as observers. Each member of the group is given a blank sheet of paper, and is asked to write the following information on it – it is wise to take this in steps as set out below. They must be told at the start that the information they write down will be shared, so that anything too personal which they would not wish to be generally known should be omitted.

(a) In the middle of the sheet their name, the name they wish to be known by on the course.

In each of the four corners of the paper:

(b) the person's occupation (or some other relevant piece of information to do with their work setting)
(c) a significant person in her or his life other than a member of the immediate family
(d) a significant event in her or his life
(e) her or his aims in coming on the course.

(Other information can be substituted if the tutor prefers.)

(f) In the four spaces between their name and the four corners the group member is asked to write up to four hobbies or interests.

The group is then divided into pairs, with each person in the pair nominated A or B. The pairs spend 15 minutes sharing what they have written with each other.

At the end of this time the tutor collects the papers in, and ask the pairs to join up so that they make groups of four people. In the foursome each A takes a turn in introducing their partner B to the new pair for four minutes. Keeping time for this part of the exercise is essential – the tutor can call out the start and end of each four-minute period. The person being introduced is not allowed to say anything, or to correct any misinformation at the end of this introduction. If the person making the introduction does not speak for the full four minutes (which is only just over a half of the time they spent listening to each other originally!), the new pair to whom B is being introduced may ask questions about B of the speaker, who answers if he or she knows. This same procedure is followed by each B in turn introducing their partner (A) for four minutes.

After this period of 16 minutes the two As become a new pair, and the two Bs a second pair, and each new pair joins up with a different pair. The same procedure is followed in these new sets of four, although this time only two minutes is allowed for each introduction – again the time needs to be strictly kept, and again questions can be asked if the person introducing their partner dries up before the end of the time allotted to them.

At the end of this period the whole group should discuss the exercise, or it can initially be discussed in the original pairings: what did it feel like to have to remember different conversations? What did it feel like to be talked about, or to hear information that was or became distorted, etc.? Frequently there is much misinformation passed on by the end of the exercise, which often occurs in listening in helping situations too, especially when the helper is told by the client about a third party. We also tend to hear what we want to hear, and not what the other wishes us to know.

Notes

1. Introducing the Basic Guidelines

1. These and other materials, audio-visual, videotapes and overhead projector slides, are available from the Department of Adult Education, Vaughan College, St Nicholas Circle, Leicester LE1 4LB. Please send s.a.e. for details, making quite clear the nature of the request.
2. I refer to such qualities in my book *Still Small Voice* (SPCK 1993), particularly Chapters 4 and 5.

2. Guidelines for Listening

1. Available for sale or hire from Audio-Visual Services, PO Box 138, Medical Sciences Building, University of Leicester, University Road, Leicester LE1 9HN.
2. This aspect of monitoring our own reactions is part of the psycho-analytic concept of 'counter-transference', and as such is referred to in my book *Still Small Voice*, pp. 196–200.
3. D. W. Winnicott, *The Maturational Process and the Facilitating Environment* (Hogarth 1965), p. 229.
4. Ursula Le Guin, *A Wizard of Earthsea* (Puffin Books 1971), p. 29.

3. Guidelines for Responding

1. A video, *The Clumsy Counsellor*, featuring the author in a series of bad responses, to help viewers to frame better ways of handling situations is available from Audio-Visual Services, PO Box 138, Medical Sciences Building, University of Leicester, University Road, Leicester LE1 9HN.

4. Putting the Guidelines Together

1. See the companion volume in this series: S. Walrond-Skinner, *Family Matters: The Pastoral Care of Personal Relations* (SPCK 1988).

5. Advanced Facilitating Skills

1. A video, *Awkward Customers*, featuring different counsellors in a series of difficult situations, is available from Audio-Visual Services, PO Box 138, Medical Sciences Building, University of Leicester, University Road, Leicester LE1 9HN.
2. R. D. Laing, *The Divided Self* (Penguin Books 1965); H. Searles, *Collected Papers on Schizophrenia and Related Subjects* (Hogarth Press 1965).
3. For further reading on this subject, including what might make people wish to work in the helping professions or in a voluntary capacity, see M. Jacobs, *Still Small Voice*, Chapter 4, 'Starting with Yourself'.
4. This whole subject is treated more fully in *Still Small Voice*, Chapter 8, 'Meeting Resistance'.
5. This term, together with counter-transference and other aspects of the therapeutic relationship, is more fully explained in *Still Small Voice*, Chapter 9, 'The Counselling Relationship'.
6. I. D. Yalom, *Love's Executioner* (Bloomsbury 1989).
7. The quotations here and in the list below come from *Love's Executioner*, pp. 180–84.

6. Where Next?

1. P. Hawkins and R. Shohet, *Supervision in the Helping Professions* (Open University Press 1989); J. Foskett and D. Lyall, *Helping the Helpers* (SPCK 1988).
2. The British Association for Counselling, 1 Regent Place, Rugby, Warks CV21 2PJ. Web site: http//www.bac.co.uk

Further Reading

Foskett, J. and Lyall, D., *Helping the Helpers: Supervision and Pastoral Care* (SPCK 1988).

Hargie, O. (ed.), *Handbook of Communication Skills* (Routledge 1996).

Hawkins, P. and Shohet, R., *Supervision in the Helping Professions* (Open University Press 1989).

Heron, J., *Helping the Client: a Creative Practical Guide* (Sage Publications 1990).

Inskipp, F., *Skills Training for Counselling* (Cassell 1995).

Jacobs, M., *Still Small Voice* (SPCK, 2nd edn 1993).

Jacobs, M. (ed.), *The Care Guide: an Interdisciplinary Manual for the Caring Professions and other Agencies* (Cassell 1995).

Jacobs, M., *The Presenting Past: the Core of Psychodynamic Counselling and Therapy* (Open University Press, 2nd edn 1998).

Jacobs, M., *Psychodynamic Counselling in Action* (Sage Publications, 2nd edn 1999).

Kennedy, E. and Charles, S., *On Becoming a Counsellor* (Gill and Macmillan, 2nd edn 1990).

King, G., *Counselling Skills for Teachers* (Open University Press 1999).

le May, A., *Communicating with Older People* (Cassell 1997).

Mearns, D. and Thorne, B., *Person-Centred Counselling in Action* (Sage Publications 1988).

Nelson-Jones, R., *You Can Help* (Cassell 1993).

Nelson-Jones, R., *Practical Counselling and Helping Skills* (Cassell, 4th edn 1996).

Seden, J., *Counselling Skills for Social Workers* (Open University Press 1999).

Stewart, W. E. and Sutton, J., *The Art and Skill of Counselling* (Cassell 1997).

Walrond-Skinner, S., *Family Matters: the Pastoral Care of Personal Relations* (SPCK 1988).

Index

SPCK

The Society for Promoting Christian Knowledge (SPCK) was founded in 1698. It has as its purpose three main tasks:

- **Communicating the Christian faith in its rich diversity**

- **Helping people to understand the Christian faith and to develop their personal faith**

- **Equipping Christians for mission and ministry**

SPCK Worldwide serves the Church through Christian literature and communication projects in over 100 countries. Special schemes also provide books for those training for ministry in many parts of the developing world. SPCK Worldwide's ministry involves Churches of many traditions. This worldwide service depends upon the generosity of others and all gifts are spent wholly on ministry programmes, without deductions.

SPCK Bookshops support the life of the Christian community by making available a full range of Christian literature and other resources, and by providing support to bookstalls and book agents throughout the UK. SPCK Bookshops' mail order department meets the needs of overseas customers and those unable to have access to local bookshops.

SPCK Publishing produces Christian books and resources, covering a wide range of inspirational, pastoral, practical and academic subjects. Authors are drawn from many different Christian traditions, and publications aim to meet the needs of a wide variety of readers in the UK and throughout the world.

The Society does not necessarily endorse the individual views contained in its publications, but hopes they stimulate readers to think about and further develop their Christian faith.

For further information about the Society, please write to:
SPCK, Holy Trinity Church, Marylebone Road,
London NW1 4DU, United Kingdom.
Telephone: 0171 387 5282